The Model

TURBO-PROP ENGINE

FOR HOME CONSTRUCTION

The Model

TURBO-PROP ENGINE

FOR HOME CONSTRUCTION

BY KURT SCHRECKLING DIPL.-ING.

Translated from the original German by Keith Thomas

Technical support by Tom Wilkinson of the Gas Turbine Builders Contact Group

Published by Traplet Publications Limited 2000
Traplet House,
Severn Drive,
Upton-upon-Severn,
Worcestershire. WR8 0JL
United Kingdom.

ISBN 1 900371 26 X

Front Cover
The OHDIE 7 on the test ring.

Back Cover
The author with OHDIE 7 on the Kangaroo test aircraft.

TRAPLET
PUBLICATIONS

Printed and bound by Stephens & George Limited,
Merthyr Industrial Estate, Dowlais, Merthyr Tydfil, Mid Glamorgan CF48 3TD

About the Author

Kurt Schreckling was born in 1939, and his education began with basic technical studies, after which he completed a university course in applied physics. For 32 years he worked in a number of technical departments of a large chemical company. Before his fifth birthday Kurt had his first practical experience of model flying when he converted a tangled kite into a model aircraft. Some years later he started building model aircraft and developed several radio control systems.

Herr Schreckling took early retirement several months ago, and he has been enjoying his new-found free time to concentrate even harder on new forms of model power plant which he hopes to develop. Kurt would not deny that he also enjoys good food, but he remains in good health and enjoys life not only as a model flyer, but also as an experimental skier: carrying out unusual experiments relating to Centre of Gravity and snow. To date he has survived all this unharmed.

Contents

Foreword

It is just ten years since the first model jet turbine engines were produced. In the intervening period development has been extremely rapid, due primarily to the intensive work of a small number of committed amateurs. The result is that the main attractions at many of today's model flying events are the turbine-powered model jets, often present in a wide range of aircraft types. Special meetings and competitions for jet models are now held, and at such events the turbine-powered model has already assumed the dominant position.

The literature on this subject amounts to just a handful of books – unless you include publications not aimed at the normal model flyer – and for this reason it seems a good idea to present my findings to date on the development of shaft turbines designed to power models.

If our existing turbines are already so outstandingly good, we need a good reason to build new variants on the type. This is the reason: of all the full-size industrial turbine engines currently being made, the majority are used to drive shafts. The shafts in turn power helicopters, propellers, fans, electrical generators, vehicle axles and other machinery. Until now only a very small number of shaft turbines have been built to model scale, and that is why I wanted to write this book, presenting my own design of shaft turbines, developed and tested by myself, in the hope that as many modellers as possible will take up the challenge and build their own versions.

At this point I ought to warn you of a particular hazard: if you continue reading this book, you are very likely to become infected with the dreaded "turbine fever" virus. The author declines all liability for the outcome!

Chapter 1

Turbines for the non-mathematician

What is a turbine?

Even though it is ten years since the first turbine-powered model aircraft actually flew, the same question crops up again and again at flying displays: "what sort of engine is there inside a turbine, then?" The question is posed by folk who appear to think that we have cunningly hidden some special type of piston engine or even electric motor inside the turbine. Although I am not on intimate terms with every single turbine that has ever been built, I can still state without hesitation: there really is not a piston engine or electric motor inside the case! If you have absolutely no knowledge of the workings of the gas turbine, the next section is aimed squarely at you: I will attempt to explain how it works in a form which is as easily digestible as possible. Curiously, in most physics text books you will not find the term "turbine" at all. In the new Fischer dictionary we find this: "turbine: rotary motor in which the energy in a flowing medium (water, steam or gas) is converted into mechanical energy; its ancestors were windmills and water wheels . . ." In the relevant technical text books

Close to the airport of Mallorca can be seen a special type of shaft turbine engine which demonstrates that turbine technology has found practical applications for many years. In the background you can see a modern turbo-prop passenger aircraft on the landing approach.

turbines in all their variety are covered in detail under the umbrella term "flow machines".

An excellent example is the wheel of a water mill, as we can see exactly what is going on: a flow of water is directed tangentially onto the vanes mounted on the periphery of a wheel, or rotor, and this action forces the wheel to rotate. In this case it is obvious how the energy in the water affects the wheel. Note that the wheel can only be used to drive something if the force acting upon it is directed on its periphery. The energy in the flowing water is thereby transferred to the wheel or rotor, which can then perform useful work.

If the water wheel is a water turbine, it follows that a windmill or wind turbine is an "air turbine", and since air – the flowing medium – is gaseous, these machines also justify the description "gas turbine". The photograph of the wind-driven pump with the turbo-prop passenger aircraft in the background shows very clearly the wide-ranging applications of the turbine principle, even when restricted to the medium of gas.

Wind and water wheels have been in use for centuries, and they exploit the flow energy which is present in the natural world. Modern turbine engines which exploit the principle of the gas turbine use thermal energy to generate their own wind to drive turbine wheels. This means that they belong in the large category of thermal engines. In the "Dubbel" pocket book of engineering we find the following definition: "the gas turbine is a thermal engine which generates mechanical power (shaft power) or thrust (e.g. in aircraft engines) . . . " According to this definition, the term "gas turbine" can be applied to all kinds of turbo-jet and shaft turbine engines. Model turbines such as the JPX, FD, Microturbine, Turbomin, Pegasus, KJ-66 can therefore be classed as gas turbines, but so also can the OHDIE 5, 6 and 7 shaft turbine engines presented in this book, together with all the other variations on the type which already exist or will exist in the future. Many model flyers erroneously confine the term "gas turbine" to jet engines which use propane gas as fuel. That is quite simply wrong.

A turbine-propeller engine, generally abbreviated to "turbo-prop", is only one representative of the shaft turbine family. Different applications of the general principle have produced power plants which are used in helicopters, marine vessels, ground-based vehicles and also stationary plant such as pumps, compressors and electrical generators, and this list is by no means complete.

In theory, the term "turbo-motor" would certainly be appropriate to these engines, although to the layman this seems to imply a piston engine fitted with a turbo-charger. However, all shaft turbine engines have rotating compressor and turbine wheels instead of pistons and cylinders, so I shall use the shorter term "shaft turbine" in the remainder of this book to describe this specialised

Turbo-jet powered model aircraft in large numbers seen at the Whittle Ohain Trophy in the Summer of 1998. Just a few years previously it would been thought incredible that such a wide range could have been produced so soon.

species of the gas turbine genus. It is unfortunately the case that even the experts do not use the various terms logically and clearly in their everyday speech. It is therefore absolutely essential to state exactly what is meant by the word "turbine" every time it is used, otherwise the uninitiated layman will be in a constant state of confusion. Do we mean the complete engine, or the turbine wheel, or a particular turbine stage, or perhaps something else?

I shall try to take this difficulty into account in my explanation of the method of working of the individual parts of the engine.

A Fan-Trainer built by Peter Cmyral. Here the fan is driven by a piston engine. For how much longer?

Admittedly it is not that easy to remember the correct meaning of a range of new terms when you hear and try to use them for the first time. A good example of this cropped up at a model flying display in which I was participating: although the announcer was well prepared and had been thoroughly briefed, he still came to grief when trying to differentiate between the turbines and the pulse jets. The result was that my engine was announced as a "pulse jet turbine", but who knows? Maybe somebody will invent something some day which will deserve this name, although he had better take the trouble to solve the attendant noise problem at the same time. Fortunately noise is not a problem with shaft turbines which are designed appropriately for use in model aircraft.

Mass, force, work, energy, power and efficiency

It is important to have an overall understanding of the meaning of these terms as they relate to physics and technology, otherwise you will quickly become confused when we start discussing the function and application of turbine engines.

Mass is a measure of the quantity of substance of a body. Force is present all about us, for example in the form of gravity due to the gravitational pull of the Earth on our own body, or when the speed of a vehicle changes. We can see from this that a body of a given mass can produce forces of varying magnitude depending on the type of acceleration to which it is subjected. In terms of physics, "force" is defined as the product of mass and acceleration, whereby acceleration is the rate of change in velocity; velocity is defined as speed in a stated direction. For example, if a model aircraft dives vertically into the ground, its velocity changes extremely quickly, which means that its rate of acceleration is correspondingly high. This example shows that a body of low mass can still exert a considerable destructive force. Where a mass is rotating, its velocity is constantly changing, and in this situation "centrifugal forces" take effect. When a mass is repelled or ejected, the force generated is precisely what is required to produce propulsion.

In terms of physics, work is defined as force multiplied by distance, measured in the direction of travel. Energy is the capacity to execute work. This means that the natural wind possesses kinetic energy in just the same way as the exhaust flow of a jet engine.

Power is work divided by the period of time in which the work was performed. The following method of demonstrating this is extremely impressive if you try it out yourself: locate a fairly long staircase, and climb it once at your normal speed. Now try it again, moving as fast as you possibly can. The work performed in both cases is identical, if we overlook the slight increase in air resistance due to climbing at high speed. However, you will be in no doubt that you have generated more power in the high-speed climb.

The energy required to execute the work is stored in your muscles and fat reserves in the form of chemical energy. When we use the term "power" in everyday speech, it does not always mean the same as the definition used in physics, as the scientific term says nothing about the actual work performed.

If you carry out the experiment outlined above exactly as described, and then analyse the results with a little more care, you will probably come to the following realisation: not only have you performed "useful work" by climbing the staircase, but the effort has also warmed you up considerably. The "thermal engines" of your body, namely your muscles, only convert into useful work a part of the energy passed to them. The ratio of useful work to energy consumed is termed efficiency. In any energy conversion process which works constantly we can also describe the power ratio as efficiency, in which case the values are simply stated as a number or a percentage. Since there are always losses involved in

Another example for possible future turbo-fan applications: a model Harrier hovering, as demonstrated by Mike Coscela during the first jet meeting in Mallorca in 1996. The model is fitted with a conventional impeller powered by a two-stroke engine.

all energy conversion processes, efficiency is always less than 1, or smaller than 100%.

What is the equivalent in horsepower of 5 Kilopond (kp) of thrust? Questions like this are commonly expressed, and difficult to answer. The question implies that force and power are unconsciously considered to be equivalents, and the use of antiquated units such as brake horsepower (BHP) and kp do not clarify the matter. However, the confusion is also due to the fact that the performance of internal combustion engines and electric motors is usually stated in the form of shaft power, while static thrust is usually quoted for turbine engines.

There is little point in trying to draw comparisons here; after all, who wants to know what size of turbine is required to propel a model horse-drawn cart? Even fewer modellers are interested in equating the power of cart-horses with the power requirements of aircraft. EU regulations now state that, as far as possible, only SI units (SI = System International d'Unites = international system of units) should be used. According to the SI system, mass is measured in kilograms (abbreviation: kg), power in Watts, kiloWatts or megaWatts (abbreviations: W, kW, MW), force in Newtons (abbreviation: N), work and energy in Joules (J, kJ, MJ), whereby k stands for Kilo (one thousand of the stated units), M for Mega (one million of the stated units). Equally common are the prefixes Milli- (one thousandth of the unit in question), Micro- (one millionth of the unit) etc.

You may not be fully conversant with SI units, but they make good sense when it comes to carrying out calculations concerning physical and technical processes.

Applying these findings to model engines

If we are to make an attempt at answering the BHP/Kilopond question with some degree of accuracy, we need to know one extra factor: the speed of the model. For example, a perfectly practical case is that of a model aircraft held stationary on the ground for a test run, with an engine producing 50 N of static thrust. How much power is being transferred to the model? Evidently absolutely none, for although the engine is producing 50 N of thrust, it is not moving the model at all. However, the engine is nevertheless converting considerable energy per unit of time, so where is the power it is generating? Take a look at the rear of the engine, and you can see the answer very clearly: all the engine's power from the exhaust flow or from the propeller's airflow is transferred (lost) to the environment. It makes no difference whether the thrust is produced by a turbine engine or by any other form of motor with a propeller.

How about a comparison of power produced by a 50 N jet turbine and a 10 cc motor when the model is in flight? For the moment, let us assume that the model's airspeed is 180 km/hr, which corresponds to 50 m/s. At this speed the thrust of the turbine will fall slightly to 45 N. We also assume that the drag of the model is equal to the engine's thrust, but acting in the opposite direction. In this state the model moves forward steadily at a rate of 50 m every second. We can now calculate the work performed by the engine as follows:

45 N x 50 m = 2,250 Nm = 2,250 J (Joules).

The unit of time here is one second. Accordingly the engine's power is:

2,250 J/1 s = 2,250 W (Watts)

In this calculation we have worked out the engine's power as defined by work divided by time. However we can obtain the same result by measuring the aircraft's airspeed in m/s and multiplying it by the engine's thrust measured in N. From this information we can derive the following equation:

Flight power = thrust x speed.

With a standard 10 cc motor this level of power in flight

cannot be achieved, as its shaft power is only around 1,200 W. The answer to the original question is therefore as follows: at take-off the jet turbine is as powerful as a good 10 cc two-stroke, but even at 180 km/hr it is more powerful than two of these motors. We can see that this is likely to be true from a glance at the glow motor's shaft power: if it produces 1,200 W, its thrust would be 24 N, if we ignore the losses in the propeller. If we assume a propeller efficiency of 75%, the motor can only produce 18 N at the stated airspeed, or 900 W of useful power. Of course, it is perfectly possible to achieve 180 km/hr with a 10 cc motor, but in this case the drag of the model must be much lower than in our example.

How turbine wheels work

The first drawing shows the flow through an axial turbine wheel in diagrammatic form. This type of wheel is termed "axial" because the flow through it is generally in the axial direction. In practical terms, the turbine blades are completely sealed at the tip by the turbine wheel housing. The result is that the gas flow is deflected backwards at an angle, as shown in the diagram. As we have already seen, the process of changing the direction of flow in a fluid medium produces a force which acts on the periphery of the wheel. This force varies according to the change in peripheral speed and the diameter of the wheel. It is possible to amplify the effect of the force on the wheel by directing the flow accurately into the blades of the wheel, i.e. as close as possible to the wheel's direction of rotation. This is the purpose of the turbine nozzle guide vanes. The combination of the nozzle guide vane (stator) with the turbine wheel (rotor) is called a turbine stage. The power of a single stage of this type can be calculated from the peripheral speed and the peripheral force of the turbine wheel. The peripheral force is itself determined by the mass flow, and the degree to which it is diverted in the direction opposite to the direction of rotation. The effectiveness with which the nozzle guide vanes direct the flow is included in this factor. The deflection is amplified if the gas contains sufficient energy to accelerate the flow between the blades of the turbine wheel in the opposite direction to the direction of rotation.

A gas flow which moves in the axial direction relative to the wheel, whilst at the same time rotating around it, is termed a swirling flow. The peripheral force required can also be generated by a change in this swirling motion. The swirl produced in the nozzle guide vanes alone produces a peripheral force through the action of diverting the gas in the turbine blades mounted on the turbine wheel. It is equally true that a peripheral force is generated if the gas strikes the vanes of the turbine wheel in the axial direction, but is diverted in the direction opposite to the direction of rotation by the camber of the blades. Windmills demonstrate this effect quite clearly.

To obtain maximum efficiency in a single turbine stage it is ideal if the swirling motion produced by the nozzle guide vane system is reduced by the rotation of the turbine wheel to the extent that the gas flows out of the turbine wheel purely in the axial direction, i.e. free of swirl; at the same time its velocity should be as low as possible. If this can be achieved, the kinetic energy which is carried away in the gas flow is minimised.

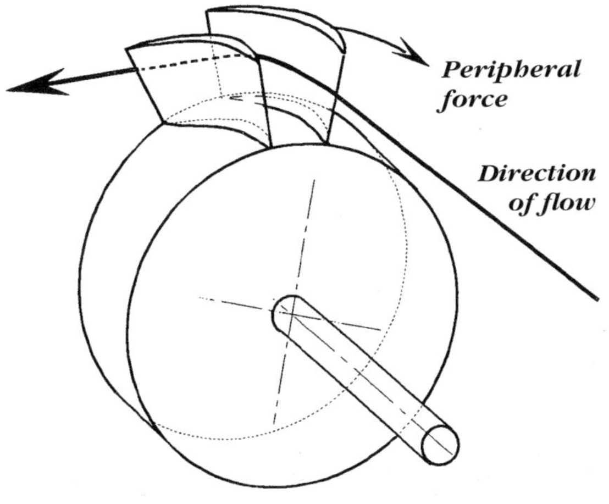

Flow through an axial turbine wheel.

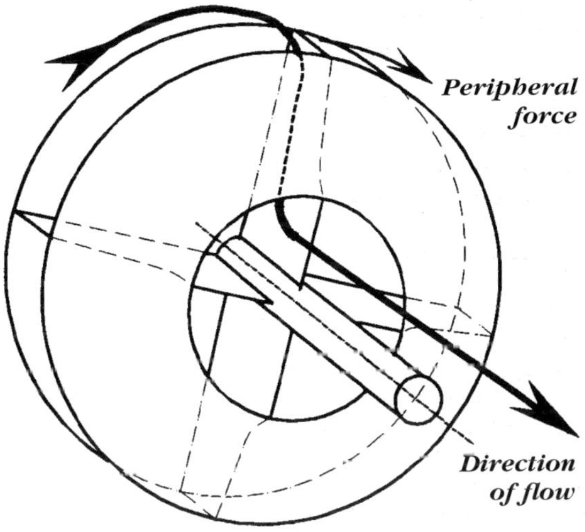

Flow through a radial turbine wheel.

However, any excess energy which has not yet been converted can be converted into shaft power in a subsequent turbine stage.

The second diagram shows the direction of flow through a radial turbine wheel. Here the change in swirl, and with it the peripheral force, as the gas flows through the wheel, occurs from the outside towards the inside, i.e. in the radial direction. This type of wheel is popular in the smaller exhaust turbo-charger, and in single-shaft turbine engines.

A peripheral force, or torque, is generated by the blades of a turbine wheel even if it does not rotate at all, provided that gas flows through it.

Chapter 2

From the jet turbine to the shaft turbine

The turbo-jet engine, more correctly known as an air turbine jet engine, is in its simplest form a pure generator of thrust. The drawing on the next page shows the basic construction and method of working of a model jet turbine. However, with relatively little effort it is possible to persuade a jet engine to transmit its power to a drive shaft, instead of producing power in the form of a jet. In concrete terms this means that we can use the technology developed for existing model jet turbines as the basis for shaft turbines, and in so doing reap many advantages.

In its simplest form such an engine can be based on any model turbo-jet you like, without internal modifications, i.e. the turbine forms the core engine for a shaft turbine. The term "gas generator" is sometimes used instead of "core engine".

Steps in converting the turbo-jet

In a turbo-jet engine all the mechanical power is released in the exhaust jet. We need to exploit the excess energy which is present in the gas as it leaves the turbine stage and enters the thrust nozzle. This is the point at which we apply our modifications:

Step 1

First we remove the thrust nozzle. This causes a very significant drop in exhaust gas temperature. However, in

This wonderful large model is simply crying out for turbo-fan engines.

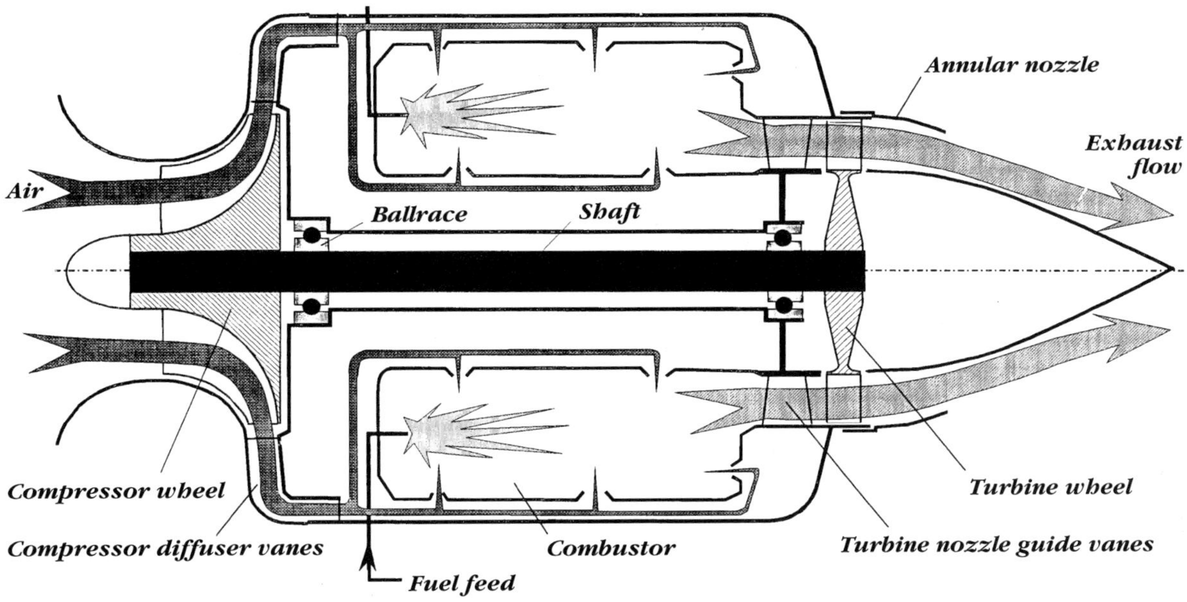

The basic method of working of a model turbo-jet engine. The compressor wheel rotates very fast, and constantly sucks in air, compresses it and feeds it into the combustor. At the same time fuel is burned and thereby increases the capacity of the gas to perform work considerably. It can now carry out more work than is required to drive the compressor wheel. The turbine wheel draws from the hot air the necessary energy to drive the compressor wheel. The excess work capacity is converted into kinetic energy in the exhaust flow as it passes through the annular nozzle. This produces the thrust which propels the model aircraft.

our experience the engine still retains 70% of its maximum thrust in this form.

Step 2

We install an exhaust diffuser in place of the exhaust nozzle. If correctly designed, the diffuser causes a further considerable fall in exhaust gas temperature. Essentially we do not need to make any further modifications to the rest of the core engine.

Step 3

We now simply couple a gearbox carrying any suitable load (e.g. a propeller) to the shaft of a turbine, as shown in the diagram overleaf. This method is employed in many "full-size" industrial shaft turbines, although it is always necessary to calculate the load very accurately, or provide a means of varying the load. However, for model applications this is too complex a solution, and therefore not feasible.

For example, if the load on the turbine is excessive, e.g. too large a propeller is fitted, the engine would overheat or even fail to start. To solve this problem a gearbox is required, in order to reduce the turbine's running speed of 120,000 r.p.m. or more to usable propeller speeds. This solution is certainly possible, but the first point, the accurate calculation of the correct load, caused me to abandon what is known as single-shaft technology for model use.

Step 4

A second turbine wheel is installed at any suitable point in the engine where either cold air or the hot gas from the core engine is flowing through. This second turbine wheel is mounted on a separate shaft – the power turbine shaft – which is designed to allow both shafts to rotate independently of each other. This system can be termed a shaft engine with free-running power turbine. A second turbine nozzle guide vane system can be used, but it is not essential.

This book describes three practical variations on this theme: OHDIE 5, OHDIE 6 and OHDIE 7. In my terms "practical" means that these engines have actually been installed in model aircraft (and even a model helicopter) and powered them in the air. It is very easy to show by theoretical calculation that shaft turbine engines with the power turbine stage at the hot end of the gas flow are much more powerful than engines with a "cold" power turbine for a given fuel consumption.

Internal efficiency, mass flow, pressure ratio, turbine intake temperature

If we wish to calculate the shaft power of a projected turbine engine – and also the thrust of a standard turbo-jet engine – we need to understand the influence of the factors listed in the title, and the way in which they are inter-connected.

Internal efficiency is a means of assessing the quality of a single compressor or turbine stage. Efficiency is stated as a numeric value in the range 70 to 80%, and significant improvements are unlikely. However, there is scope for adjusting the other factors within fairly wide limits.

Mass flow (of the air) is measured in kg/s; note that we are only concerned here with the mass flow through

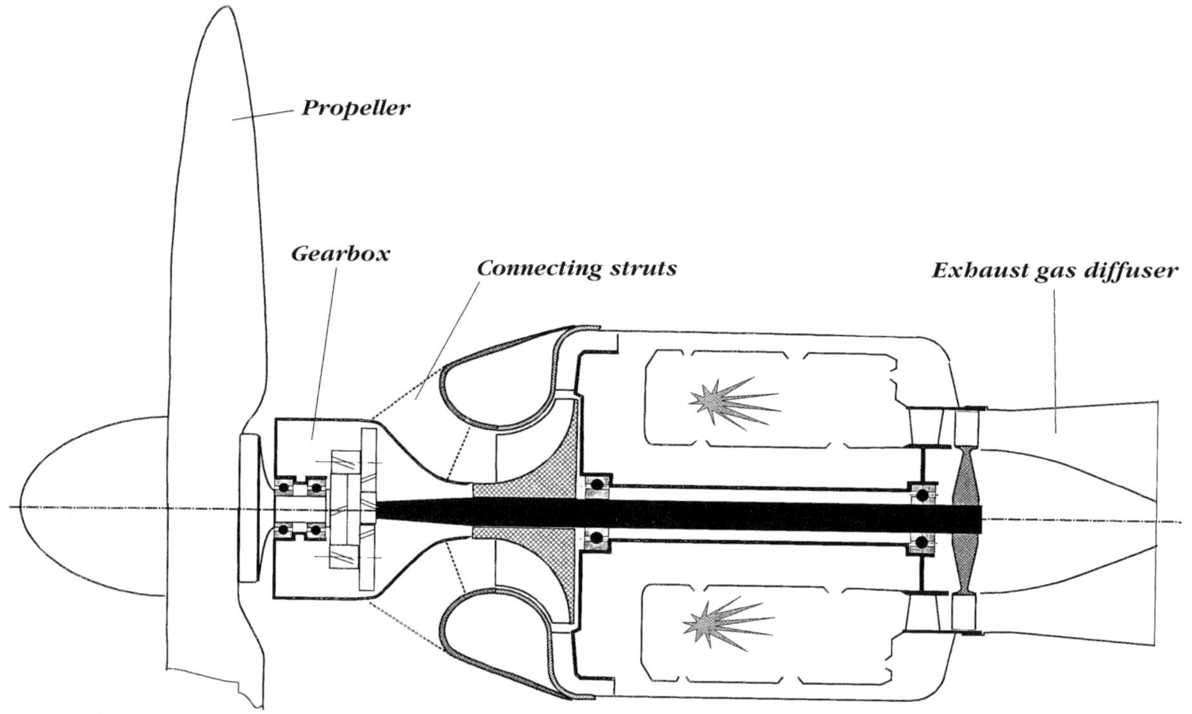

Diagram of a single-shaft turbo-prop engine.

the core engine. Typical numeric values for model turbo-jet engines are in the range 0.1 to 0.4 kg/s at full load, depending on the size of the engine.

The pressure ratio is defined as compressor pressure divided by atmospheric air pressure. For our purposes the practical top limit is a pressure ratio of up to 3.

The turbine intake temperature (abbreviation: T3) is the temperature of the gas at the point where it enters the diffuser vanes before passing to the turbine wheels. In practice the maximum temperature is 700°C if we are to continue to use normal available materials. If we allow higher temperatures, we are obliged to use extremely exotic materials and/or devise complex cooling techniques.

How much shaft power is possible? How much do we need?

This section attempts to clarify the connection between the various factors with the help of diagrams, in order to avoid the need for complex mathematical formulae. The diagrams show results which have already been calculated. Please bear in mind that my own practical experience extends back over more than ten years, so the "estimatology" used in the graphs naturally benefits from that knowledge.

It is standard practice when presenting this type of information to state the "specific power" in kW/kg, i.e. the power which an engine would generate at a nominal mass flow of 1 kg/s.

In some of the diagrams the compressor pressure is stated instead of the pressure ratio. This applies where compressor pressure can actually be measured. The following conversion formula applies in this case:\

Measured compressor pressure in bar = pressure ratio -1

This is a simplification, but it is of practical use; it only applies at sea level, as atmospheric air pressure at this altitude can be assumed to be 1 bar with reasonable accuracy. 1 bar corresponds to 1,000 hPa = 1,000 Hectopascal = 100,000 Pascal according to the SI system. Unfortunately I have not seen an affordable pressure gauge calibrated using this unit of measurement which is suitable for the typical modeller. Compressor pressure can be measured in the casing at a point just downstream of the compressor diffuser vanes.

Let us now examine diagram 1. Example A shows the data for the KJ-66 turbo-jet engine. It shows a point on the graph corresponding to a maximum pressure of 1.2 bar, i.e. a pressure ratio of 2.2. For the moment we will assume that this engine has already been converted to form a core engine. If this is the case, we can read off a specific power of 37 kWs/kg air throughput. The actual air throughput is 0.24 kg/s. These figures can now be used to calculate the actual shaft power of such an engine:

0.24 kg/s x 37 kWs/kg = 8.88 kW

Example B shows the case for a core engine in which the turbine intake temperature is artificially kept low, as it assumes that a turbine wheel for a small engine capable of surviving in very high temperatures is simply not available. For this reason the maximum pressure is restricted to 0.7 bar, i.e. the peripheral speed of the wheels is limited, and a turbine intake temperature of only 600°C is permitted. The diagram shows that the engine's specific power under such conditions is 22.8 kWs/kg. This means that a small shaft turbine with an air throughput of only 0.075 kg/s would generate a shaft power of:

0.075 kg/s x 22.8 kWs/kg = 1.71 kW.

This is already considerably more than a normal 10 cc two-stroke is capable of producing.

If we are able to use a turbine wheel with the same strength as that employed in the larger jet turbine, then we can apply the same limits relating to pressure and temperature, and therefore obtain the same level of specific power. The mass throughput of the small engine would then automatically rise to about 0.11 kg/s due to the higher power of the compressor, and in this case even the small core engine would suffice for a shaft power of more than 4 kW.

It is also possible to estimate the shaft power which can be achieved once the turbo-jet engine has been converted into a shaft turbine by making a calculation based on its jet power. Under static running conditions the jet power is: half mass flow in kg/s multiplied by jet velocity squared.

Example A shows that the KJ-66 provides 75 N thrust at a mass flow of 0.24 kg/s. Thrust divided by mass flow produces the clear answer:

Jet velocity = 312.5 ms

and from the above equation we find that:

Jet power = 11.7 kW!

With a little effort it is possible to convert around 70% of this 11.7 kW into shaft power. This means that a perfectly standard model jet turbine can be converted to generate 8.2 kW of shaft power; a figure which corresponds quite well with the 8.88 kW calculated from diagram 1.

Question: do any of us need such levels of power in our model aircraft, boats or ground based vehicles? Anyone with a little practical experience with piston engines and propellers as used in models will know that a power output of 8 kW is the sort of figure obtained only with extremely large engines. A 10 cc engine generates a shaft power of between 1 and 1.5 kW, which the propeller converts into a static thrust of 40 to 50 N. Four engines of this size provide plenty of power for a large model aircraft with a mass of close to 20 kg (more than 20 kg is not permissible in Germany in any case). A single 10 cc two-stroke motor produces adequate power for a model helicopter with a take-off mass of 10 kg.

This information shows that a core engine for a shaft turbine could reasonably be much smaller than the model turbo-jet engines currently in widespread use.

A unique implementation of the micro-turbine by Thomas Kamps: a controllable vertical take-off machine, demonstrated during the Whittle Ohain Trophy meeting in the Summer of 1998. In the background can be seen an experimental model aircraft designed as a test-bed for turbo-jet engines.

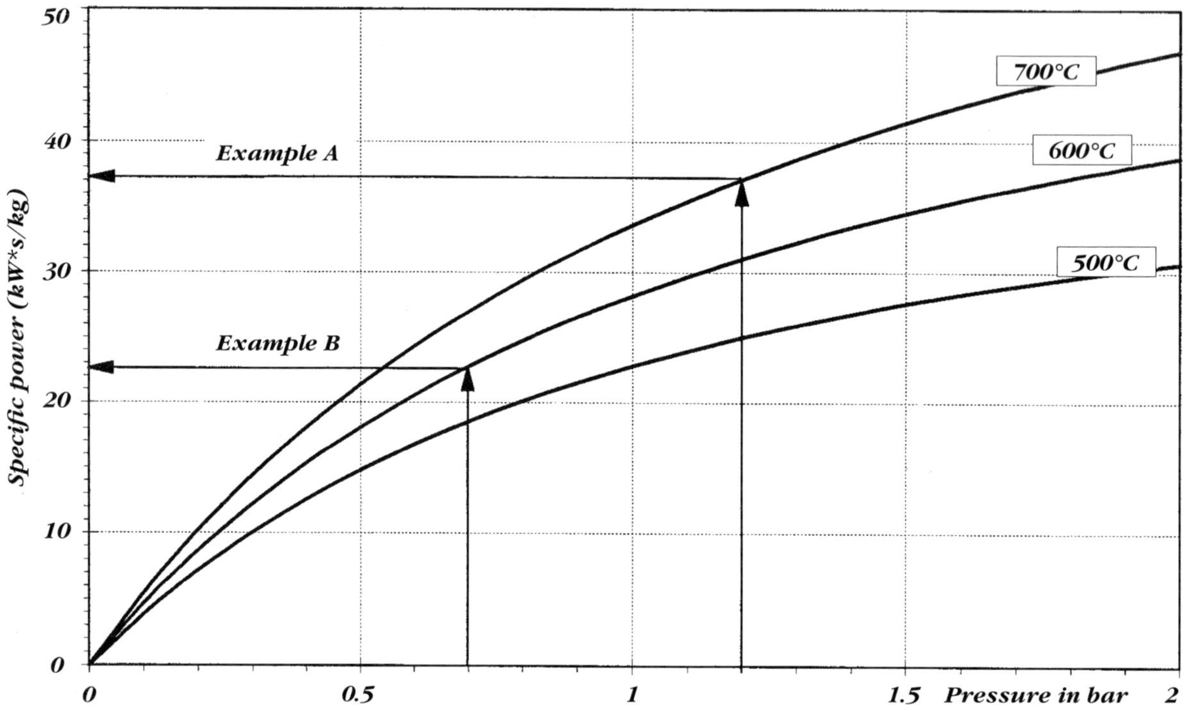

Diagram 1
Specific power varying with compressor pressure and turbine intake temperature.

Of course, it is possible to take the shaft turbine capable of 8.88 kW and throttle it back so that it generates only 4 kW, i.e. run it at lower pressure and a correspondingly reduced rotational speed. However, the relatively large engine would consume more fuel than a smaller one, which means that the model aircraft would have to carry an undesirably high load due to the extra weight of the larger engine, and the larger fuel supply required for a given operating time. The idle power of the larger engine is also inevitably higher than is desirable, and it is already too high for comfort with many relatively small models under certain circumstances. The power requirement for model boats and land-based vehicles is in any case much lower than we need for model aircraft.

Chapter 3

Operating characteristics of shaft turbines

At this point we will only discuss shaft engines with "free-running" power turbines, whose core engines are very similar to the familiar turbo-jet engines used in models, fitted with only one supplementary turbine stage.

Characteristics of the core engine

The thermal efficiency of any turbine engine improves steadily with increasing rotational speed, due to the rise in compression ratio. The engine's power capacity rises at a much higher rate than its rotational speed. If rotational speed is doubled, pressure is at least quadrupled – provided that we stay within the permissible speed range. Unfortunately these engines all too easily "forget" the limits which are laid down by the rotational speed strength of the rotating components. If the fuel flow is not governed, the engine self-destructs. It is therefore absolutely essential in every case to ensure that the engine is never supplied with too much fuel.

The bottom end of the engine's speed scale is set by what is known as the sustain speed. Below this speed the power produced by the compressor turbine wheel is too low to overcome the friction losses of the bearings at temperatures which the engine can tolerate. For safety reasons the "idle speed" is usually set at three times the sustain speed. For the OHDIE 7 engine with a compressor diameter of 50 mm the speed range which is of practical use currently lies between 40,000 and 130,000 r.p.m. The acceleration time from idle to full speed is around three seconds, although the core engine turbine accelerates fairly slowly at the bottom end of the

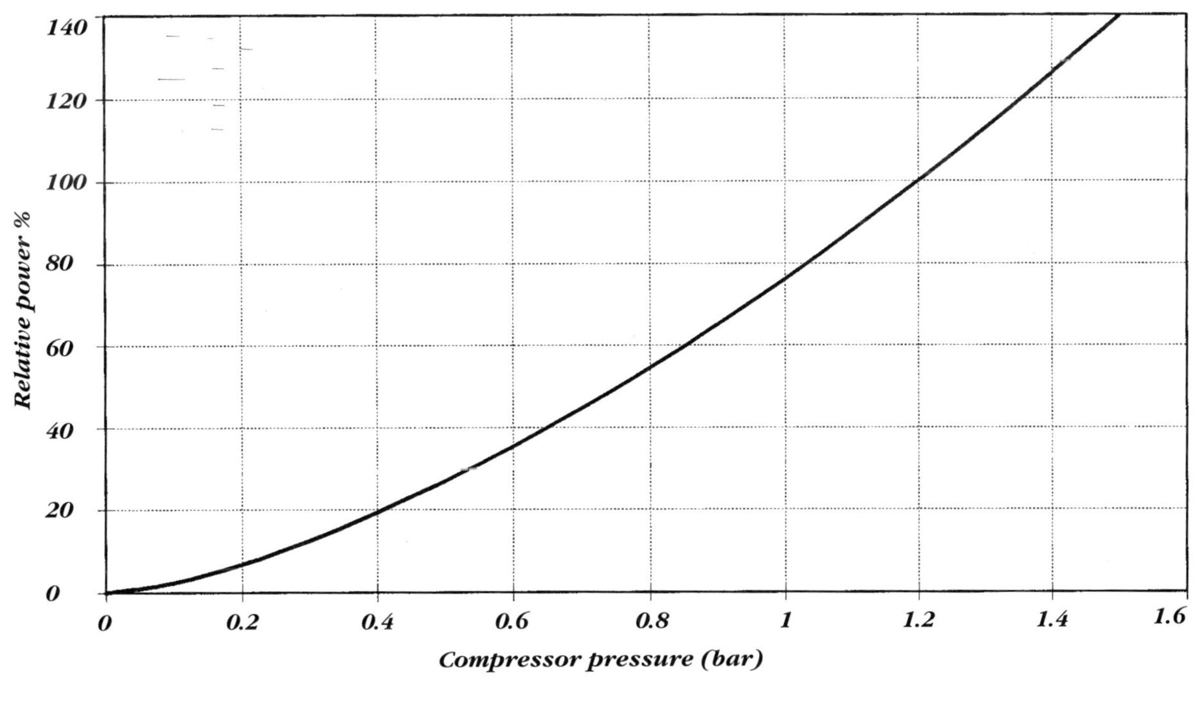

Diagram 2
Relative rise in power varying with compressor pressure.

speed range. Feeding excessive fuel to the engine at this time leads to spitting and overheating. This rotational speed range corresponds to a usable compressor pressure range of 0.1 to 0.7 bar. Since it is relatively difficult to measure rotational speed accurately, it is usual to monitor compressor pressure to ensure that the limit range is not exceeded. Diagram 2 shows the relative rise in the engine's power capacity. In this case a compressor pressure of 1.2 bar is set as the full throttle point; this corresponds to a pressure ratio of 2.2.

Note that a core engine turbine wheel has to be highly heat-resistant if this value is to be reached in practice.

Characteristics of the power turbine stage, reciprocal effects on the core engine

The extent to which the power capacity of the core engine can actually be exploited depends to a very great extent on the design (i.e. size) of the power turbine stage, and on careful selection of the load, e.g. in the form of the appropriate size of propeller. Since the hot air expands as it flows through the turbine stages, the power turbine wheel must always be larger than the turbine wheel of the core engine. A common feature of all turbine engines is that the lion's share of the engine's power capacity is absorbed in driving the compressor. In very coarse terms ¾ of the engine's power is passed back to the compressor, and the remainder is exploited in the power turbine. It is therefore always the case that the rotational speed of the power turbine is much lower than that of the compressor turbine wheel. In our engines the usable range is 0 to 40,000 r.p.m.; the latter value is the optimum speed at full throttle. If the rotational speed of the power turbine is 0 r.p.m., the power turbine shaft is stationary, and no shaft power is produced. In fact, experience shows that the core engine nevertheless continues to run happily in this situation, although the running temperature is at a maximum.

If the power turbine is left undisturbed, its rotational speed rises and falls with compressor pressure, although the scale is not linear. The core engine produces torque at the power turbine wheel even if the latter is prevented from spinning. In actual fact, the torque of the power turbine wheel is at its highest when stalled, and this is a very important practical point. For example, it is permissible to hold a propeller or helicopter rotor stationary to prevent it rotating while you start the engine, and there is no risk of damage to the core engine when you do this. The same applies if a propeller is stalled due to ground contact.

Available shaft power with a mismatched load

We will assume that the core engine is running at an approximately constant speed. We have already

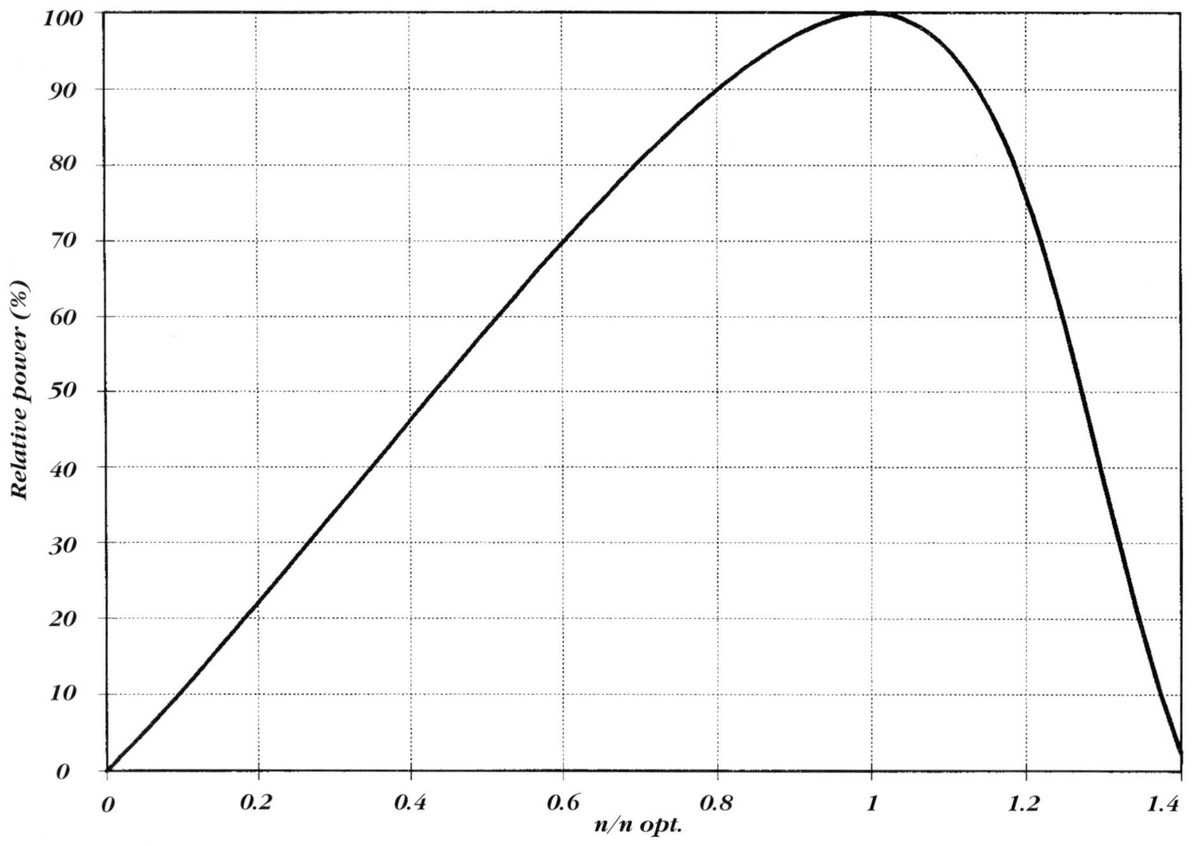

Diagram 3
Decline in power of a power turbine stage due to mismatching.

examined one extreme case, namely a stalled power turbine shaft. In this situation the shaft's torque is at a maximum, but it is incapable of supplying power.

The other extreme case is when the turbine wheel is spinning so fast that gas flows through it without being deflected. In practice this occurs if there is no load on the secondary shaft, i.e. shaft power is zero, rotational speed is maximum.

Somewhere between these two extremes lies the optimum speed, i.e. the rotational speed at which the power turbine wheel generates maximum power. This requires that the load, e.g. a propeller, is accurately matched to this rotational speed.

The practical significance of this is that the gearbox reduction ratio must be selected carefully to suit each application. In practice it is not always possible to match the load as accurately as we might wish.

In approximate terms we are able to calculate the extent to which the engine's actual usable power differs from its maximum power, if, for example, the propeller we select is larger than the optimum size. A study of diagram 3 shows this clearly. For example, if we assume that the load is so large that it limits the rotational speed of the power turbine wheel to around 60% of its optimum speed, we can see from the graph that only 70% of maximum shaft power is available. If we "strangle" the engine to such an extent that the secondary shaft is turning at only 20% of its optimum rotational speed, there is still 23% of maximum shaft power available. Let us now examine the opposite problem: if the load is too small, the power turbine wheel spins faster, but its power output is reduced. The graph shows that relative power declines fairly steeply at high rotational speeds. The power lost due to mismatching is retained in the exhaust gas, thereby producing an increase in exhaust gas velocity and/or exhaust gas temperature. This characteristic dynamic behaviour is fundamentally different to that of a piston engine: the torque of the piston engine rises with rotational speed until it reaches an optimum value. It is obvious that this type of motor produces no torque when it is at a standstill. A more relevant comparison to the shaft turbine is an electric D.C. motor. Like the turbine, the electric motor's torque is also at a maximum when the motor is stalled (shaft stationary), although in this case the situation must be avoided at all costs unless you wish to see the motor smoke itself to death; fortunately for us, this does not occur with the power turbine.

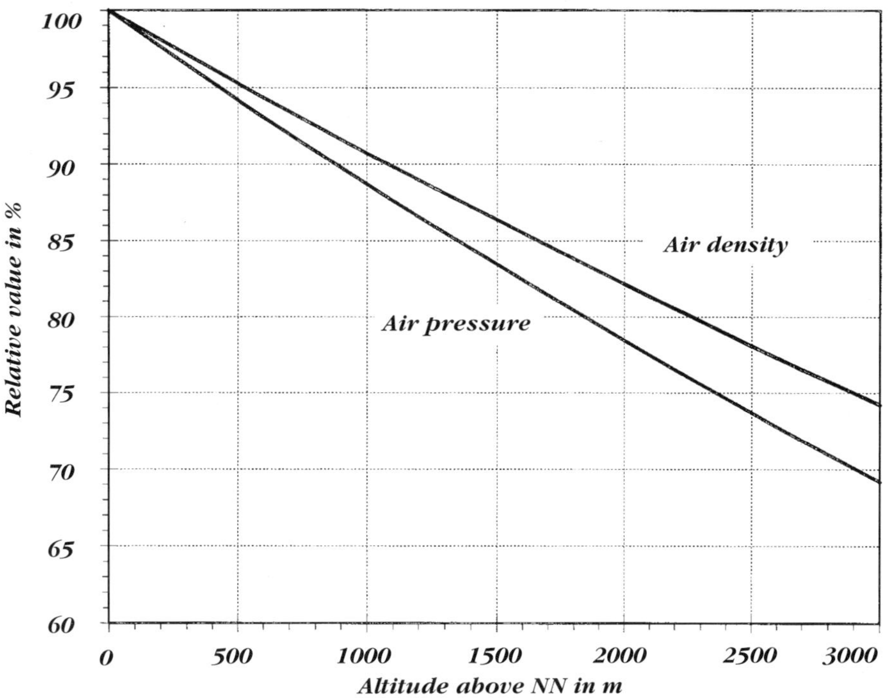

Diagram 4
Reduction in air pressure and air density with increasing altitude.

Influence of weather and site altitude

When you are operating a turbine engine it is important to take air temperature and pressure into consideration. Let us consider first the situation of normal atmospheric pressure (exactly 1,013 hPa = 1.013 bar). If we now change the temperature of the air entering the engine by 1°C, the effect is a change of around 3°C at the turbine intake, in the same direction as the original change. If the nominal ambient temperature is 15°C, then at 30°C in the shade the air temperature in the sun close to the ground may be 40°C or even higher. In this situation the blades of the core engine turbine wheel will be around 75°C hotter than under normal conditions, and at the same time the compression ratio is significantly reduced due to the higher intake temperature. In these circumstances, if we now run up the core engine to the nominal pressure calculated for normal conditions, that pressure can only be achieved by running the compressor (and its turbine wheel) at higher speed. The turbine wheel is now running at higher speed and higher temperature than its design allows, and this can easily be the last straw. The remedy is therefore to reduce the permissible maximum pressure of the engine in hot conditions. A useful guideline is this: for each degree Celsius higher than the normal temperature of 15°C, reduce the maximum pressure of the compressor by 1% by reducing the fuel supply. If the ambient temperature is lower than nominal, you are on the safe side in any case, and no correction is necessary. Of course, these rules only apply strictly when atmospheric conditions are compared with what is termed the International Standard Atmosphere (ISA). The physical values of the ISA are defined as follows:

Air pressure:	101.3 kPa (corresponding to 1,013 mbar or 1.013 bar)
Temperature:	15°C
Density:	1.225 kg/m^3

Weather conditions may cause the atmospheric pressure at a particular location to vary by around +/–5% from the average pressure, but in practice this is not especially critical. However, this is not the case if the site location is at a high altitude. Diagram 4, calculated with the help of the international altitude formula, shows the average percentage reduction in air density and in air pressure with rising altitude. The 100% value corresponds to ISA. For example, at an altitude of 1,000 m we find that air pressure is only 88.6% of that at sea level, and air density is reduced to 90.8%. These values indicate that at 1,000 m altitude the power of a piston engine – and of a shaft turbine – will decline to 90.8% of the value under normal conditions.

To find out the exact situation, we have to measure the air pressure and temperature at the site itself, and use the gas laws to calculate the actual air density. However, for practical model flying a rough guide is quite sufficient: for a given rotational speed, shaft power falls by 10% with each 1,000 m of altitude, provided that air temperature does not vary significantly from the nominal 15°C. This implies that you should reduce compressor pressure by 10% in order to stay within the rotational speed limits of the turbine.

On its own, a difference in atmospheric pressure has no significant effect on turbine intake temperature. There are a number of high-altitude locations in the world where model turbo-jet engines have been flown successfully, e.g. in the vicinity of Mexico City, at an altitude of 2,500 m, although the operators did take the trouble to familiarise themselves with the guidelines mentioned here, and applied them as required.

The unavoidable effect of the reduction in air density due to increasing altitude is to reduce the maximum power of all types of internal-combustion engine, and this includes shaft turbines. When a piston engine or a turbine is turning at a given rotational speed, the volume of air sucked into it remains constant, regardless of altitude. However, the work capacity of any internal combustion engine is dependent upon the mass flow. Since the density of the air is lower, the mass flow is reduced, and maximum power falls.

However, there is an important difference between piston engines and turbo-prop engines in their altitude-dependent behaviour: the shaft power of the piston engine declines at the same rate as the drag of the propeller as it moves through the air. As a result, the engine's rotational speed stays more or less constant with increasing altitude. However, this is not quite the full story, as internal friction losses, which vary with rotational speed, cause available shaft power to decline slightly faster than the drag of the propeller. As a result the rotational speed of the engine must fall steadily with increasing altitude. An extra complication is that, if the motor is to produce maximum power, the carburettor must be adjusted to ensure that virtually the full oxygen content of the air is exploited for combustion. For this reason it is also impossible to over-rev an engine just by setting the carburettor incorrectly.

In contrast, the turbo-prop engine does not possess a self-limiting mechanism in the combustion chamber; instead the externally metered fuel supply determines the power level. Under normal conditions the engine burns only a small proportion (around 25-30%) of the oxygen in the air which passes through the engine, and this helps to maintain the operating temperature of the highly stressed turbine wheel within tolerable limits. However, if we set the fuel feed correctly at sea level, then run the turbine at a higher altitude, the engine automatically spins much faster. This can be calculated, and the effect is as follows: at an altitude of 1,000 m the engine's rotational speed would already be around 6% higher than at sea level for a given rate of fuel delivery. Although shaft power would be the same as that generated at sea level, the engine's speed would already be in the yellow/red "danger" sector.

Naturally the reduction in air pressure, or more accurately the reduction in air density, also produces a reduction in lift generated by the model aircraft's wing. This means that the take-off speed must be correspondingly higher, and at the same time less thrust is available. The net result is that the take-off run to lift-off is necessarily longer. As a rough guide we can assume that for every 100 m of additional altitude the take-off run will be 2 to 3% longer. This problem applies equally to large and small aircraft. However, since turbine engines inherently possess relatively high reserves of power, this presents no fundamental problems.

Residual thrust

The laws of physics dictate that it is not practical to reduce the exhaust gas velocity to the ideal level after the gas leaves the power turbine stage, and this means that a proportion of the work capacity of the exhaust gas is inevitably forfeited. However, when a turbine is used as a turbo-prop engine the loss is not that significant, as the "wasted" exhaust gas produces a small amount of thrust in the required direction, i.e. the direction of flight. The residual thrust of the OHDIE 7 engine has been measured at around 5 N.

Chapter 4

Guidelines

Matching the turbo-prop engine to the propeller or helicopter rotor

As we have discovered in the previous chapter, the potential power of shaft turbine engines is high enough to compete with conventional internal combustion engines for use in models. We have also seen that the rotational speed of the power turbine shaft, at around 40,000 r.p.m., is considerably higher than is usual with the propellers employed on model aircraft. The situation is the same with full-size aircraft, and the same solution needs to be adopted: a suitable gearbox has to be installed between the power turbine shaft and the propeller. It is important to select the appropriate reduction ratio for the gearbox, and this requires us to look a little more closely at the optimum propeller to suit the model and the shaft power available. This is a subject which deserves a book by itself; the book would be a heavyweight tome, and nobody would read it. For this reason I will restrict myself here to a few crucial considerations, and attempt to clarify the situation with the help of diagrams.

The first step is to determine how much thrust the model requires, and the shaft power and propeller that are necessary to achieve this. Let us look at diagram 5. The numbers on the individual curves relate to propeller diameter in centimetres. It is obvious that the static thrust of a particular propeller rises with increasing shaft power.

Larger propellers generate more static thrust for a given level of shaft power. Now let us consider the example indicated by the arrows in diagram 5.

Starting from a shaft power of 1 kW we take a vertical line into the middle area between curves 30 and 35, i.e. we select a propeller with a diameter of 32.5 cm. Then we take a horizontal line to the left to meet the static thrust axis. There we read off 42 N. That is a guideline, and indicates how much static thrust we can expect at a shaft power of 1 kW and the propeller diameter we have selected. This is not a completely random example, as it serves as a good basic comparison with a 10 cc motor, which is often used with propellers of this diameter. The curves in the diagram apply to propellers of average pitch, i.e. with a ratio of pitch to diameter of 0.5 to 0.7. In practice, two- and three-bladed propellers of the same diameter produce essentially the same static thrust with the same shaft power, but propellers with an unusually high pitch:diameter ratio will be significantly below the curves printed here.

The 160 cm curve represents a helicopter rotor, and applies to a helicopter motor of the same capacity. From the diagram we can read off the information that this rotor supplies no less than 83 N of vertical thrust even at a shaft power of just 1 kW. This would cope with a helicopter with a take-off mass of more than 8 kg.

This diagram appears to show that the diameter of the propeller is not particularly crucial. Provided that the static thrust is sufficient to get the model into the air in the first place, one could, for example, select a higher-pitch propeller with the aim of achieving maximum possible top speed. However, we must always consider the load which is placed on the propeller by the turbine's rotational speed. Most modern propellers are supplied with the manufacturer's figures regarding maximum permissible load. Experience tells us that the propeller's rotational speed in flight is substantially

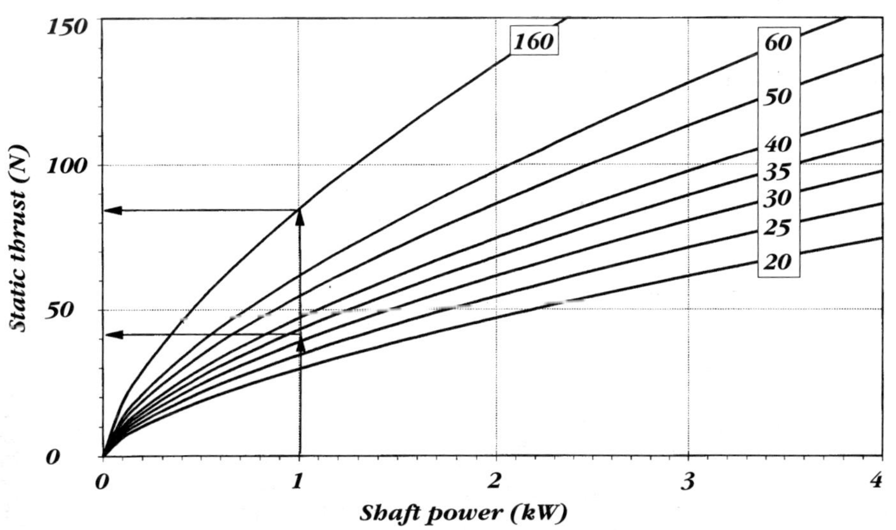

Diagram 5
Shaft power, propeller diameter, static thrust.

higher than when running on the test stand. For this reason it is important to establish the potential rotational speed of the propeller in practical flying conditions, i.e. at fairly high speed.

Diagram 6 provides the necessary guidelines. Let us take our 32 cm diameter propeller again, combined with a shaft power of 1 kW. Curves D 1 kW to D 4 kW indicate the rotational speeds at the corresponding shaft powers, i.e. 1 to 4 kW. At a shaft power of 1 kW this propeller will reach a rotational speed of 10,800 r.p.m. in flight. If we move up to the curve U 1 kW, which shows the propeller's peripheral speed at 1 kW, we can read off a peripheral speed of 182 m/s on the right-hand axis. If we were to drive the same propeller at 3 kW, then its rotational speed in flight would rise to 15,500 r.p.m., and the peripheral speed to 262 m/s. This tip speed is so high that it would cause most of the glass fibre reinforced plastic propellers in common use to fly to pieces.

This shows that, if we actually want to exploit a shaft power of 3 kW in a model aircraft in a responsible manner, we should either select a propeller which is capable of withstanding such stresses, or – preferably – use a larger three-bladed or four-bladed propeller. The rotational speed of typical three- and four-bladed propellers is slightly lower, which means a corresponding reduction in tip speed.

Even so, we must be sure to stay within the permissible limits as stated by the propeller manufacturer. For a given blade profile and shaft power, the rotational speed of a three-bladed propeller is around 13% lower than that of a two-bladed propeller of the same size, and for a four-bladed propeller the figure is around 20% lower.

Once we have established the desired rotational speed of the propeller, taking into account the maximum permissible load, all we need to do to calculate the appropriate gearbox reduction ratio is to determine the rotational speed of the power turbine shaft at the shaft power we require. The reduction ratio is then simply the rotational speed of the power turbine shaft divided by the rotational speed of the propeller. If we design the gearbox for optimum flying speed using the procedure outlined here, there will inevitably be a mismatch when the model is at rest. However, as we have discovered in the chapter "Operating characteristics of shaft turbines" in the section entitled "Available shaft power with a mismatched load", this is of no great significance for the design of the power system. Further details on practical aspects of this subject can be found in the sections "OHDIE 6" and "OHDIE 7" in the Chapter entitled "Three shaft turbine engines with free-running power turbines".

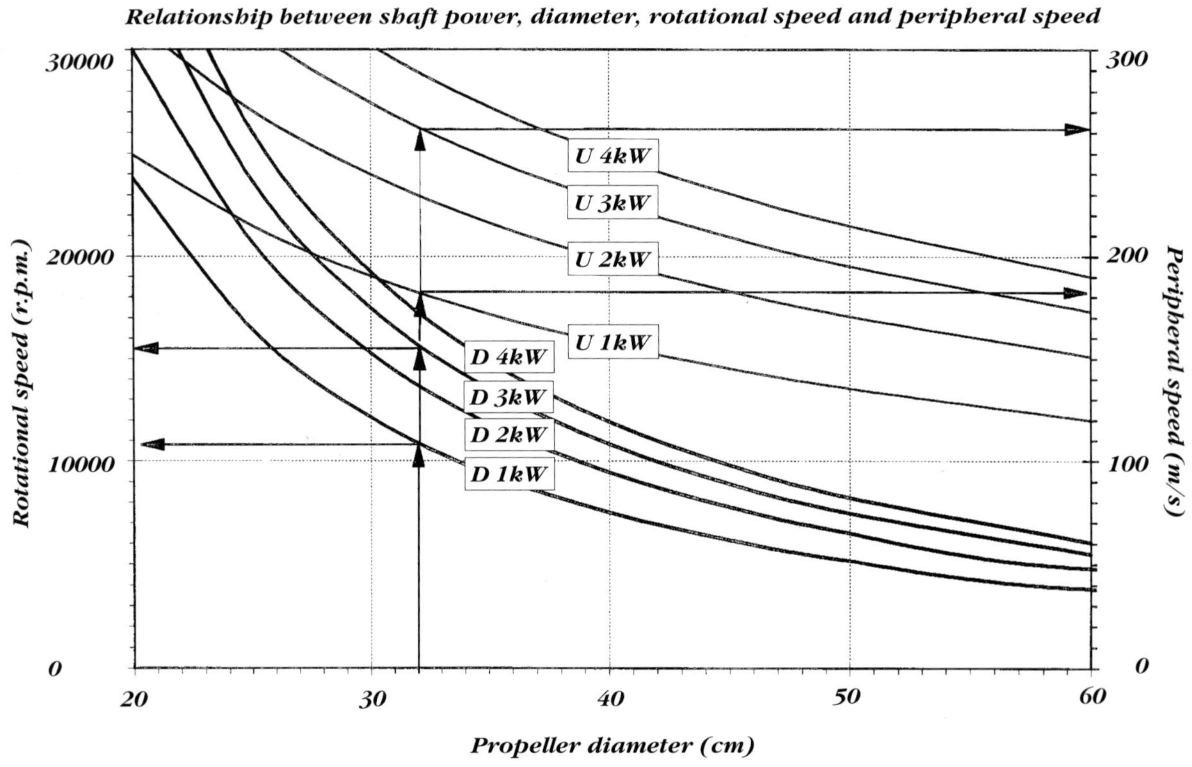

Diagram 6
Propeller at optimum airspeed.

Chapter 5

The Turbo-fan

Fan engines at model size have been popular for some time; they are known as impeller power systems or ducted fans, and are powered by two-stroke and electric motors. They are used to power model aircraft which are traditionally known as model jets. In full-size aviation turbo-fans are power plants based on shaft turbines, and they are now very commonly employed on passenger aircraft. In the model world a number of extremely large models of passenger airliners have already been built, powered by turbo-jet engines, but real model turbo-fans would undoubtedly be closer to "true scale".

Of course, the first question is the thrust which such an engine could be expected to produce. A fan accelerates a much greater quantity of air than the core engine which drives it. The ratio of the airflow through the fan relative to the airflow through the core engine is termed the by-pass ratio.

The higher the by-pass ratio, the higher the static thrust in comparison with a turbo-jet of the same size as the core engine on which it is based. Diagram 7 shows the relationship here: a by-pass ratio of 0 corresponds to a pure turbo-jet engine, and therefore represents the reference value for our purposes. If the by-pass ratio is 6, we can see that the static thrust is doubled. For example, a core engine which produces 50 N of static thrust in turbo-jet form will generate a static thrust of 100 N as a turbo-fan engine. At the same time the fuel consumption would be the same for both engines (and, incidentally, the noise level would be drastically reduced, as is the case with full-size aircraft engines). The curve shown in diagram 7 has been calculated from practical experiments, and shows the unavoidable losses in the power conversion process, which have already been taken into account. This also explains why there is a reduction in thrust if the by-pass ratio is very low, i.e. between 0 and 1.

We can consider a turbo-prop engine as a turbo-fan with a very high by-pass ratio.

Here again we are faced with the problem of matching the fan to the shaft power of the engine. Diagram 8 is intended to clarify this relationship. As with propellers, theoretical considerations show that the static thrust of a fan is fundamentally determined by the available shaft power and the efflux nozzle diameter. Here again we assume ISA. The unavoidable losses in the fan system have been taken into account in calculating the curves shown on the graph. For example, the graph shows that a fan with a diameter of 125 mm at a shaft power of 1,500 W delivers a static thrust of 40 N. This size of fan is typical of high-performance ducted fan power systems designed for use with two-stroke engines.

It is not as easy to calculate the rotational speed of the fan at the stated power level as it is with a conventional propeller. Commercially available fans of this size are designed for fan speeds in the range 18,000 to 24,000 r.p.m. The shaft power of the two-stroke engines (10-15 cc) designed to power them can be assumed to lie in the range 2 kW to 5 kW. The shaft turbine also produces around the same level of power, albeit at an optimum rotational speed (of the power turbine shaft) of around 40,000 r.p.m. This indicates that

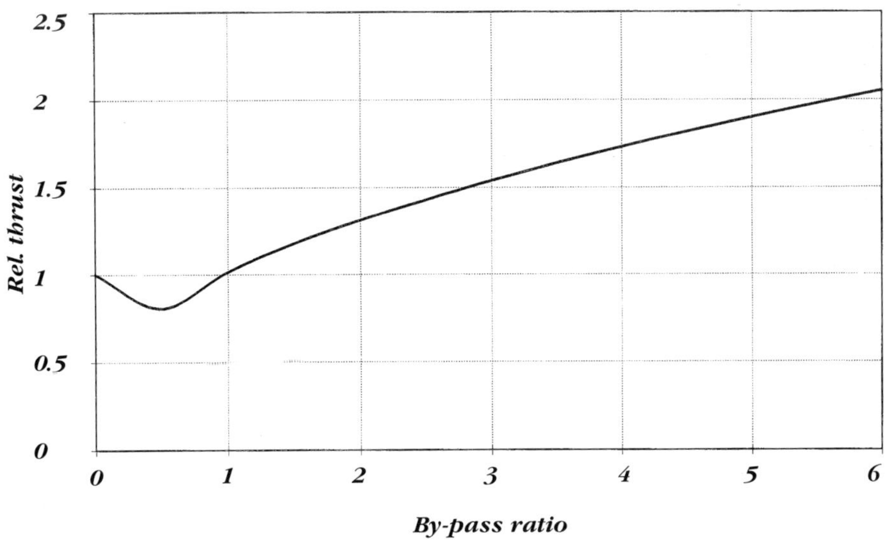

Diagram 7
Turbo-fan, thrust increase relative to turbo-jet engine, varying with by-pass ratio.

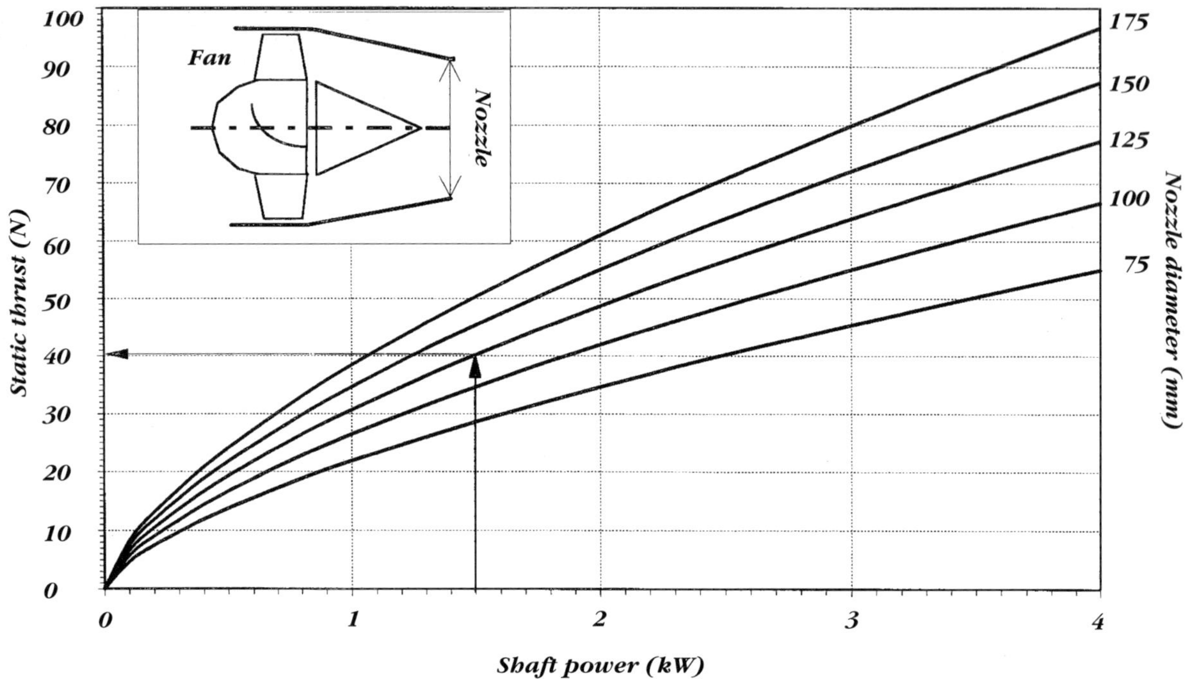

Diagram 8
Fan engine: static thrust, shaft power, nozzle diameter.

the obvious solution is once again to employ a reduction gearbox. Results of initial test-bench experiments have already confirmed the feasibility of this concept.

However, there is another potential method of avoiding the need for a gearbox, and it has been shown to be a practical solution within certain limits:

Step 1

Use a standard fan without a gearbox, coupled directly to the power turbine shaft. The inevitable mismatch of this system means that less shaft power will be available than the maximum possible.

Step 2

Design and build a fan which is designed for higher rotational speeds. This works if you reduce the pitch of the fan blades. The first test-flights have already been carried out, with successful results, and the principle appears to be practical up to a fan diameter of 180 mm. If the fan diameter is greater than this, the peripheral speed of the fan blades would be too high, so a gearbox is essential for fans of larger diameter. This is a field which certainly deserves further development.

Chapter 6

Fuel

Fuel requirements

Model turbo-jet engines are now familiar power plants, and they are not very discriminating when it comes to fuel quality. As you might expect, the shaft turbines based on them share this characteristic. In simple terms you might say that any flammable liquid can be used provided that its viscosity is no higher than that of diesel fuel.

Of all the available fuels, diesel, and similar liquids such as kerosene and paraffin, exhibit in general terms the highest calorific value, and are therefore the ideal choice as turbine fuels. Kerosene of the Jet A 1 type is designed to be used as aircraft fuel, and has a precisely defined composition; for this reason it is generally the fuel of choice for our engines.

If Jet A 1 is difficult to procure, paraffin is a good choice. It is fairly expensive, but it is the closest relative to kerosene.

In my experience the ideal compromise fuel consists of diesel or bio-diesel, with an addition of 15 to 20% of standard petrol. The petrol content improves the idling characteristics of turbine engines, but it is not absolutely essential. Pure standard petrol can also be used, but it has a slightly lower calorific value than diesel fuel per unit volume. It can also give rise to potentially explosive air-petrol vapour mixtures under unfavourable conditions.

Supplements to turbine fuel designed to increase power simply do not exist; if you want more power, just burn more fuel. The power limits are defined by the laws of physics, the technical design of the engine, and the characteristics of the materials used in its construction.

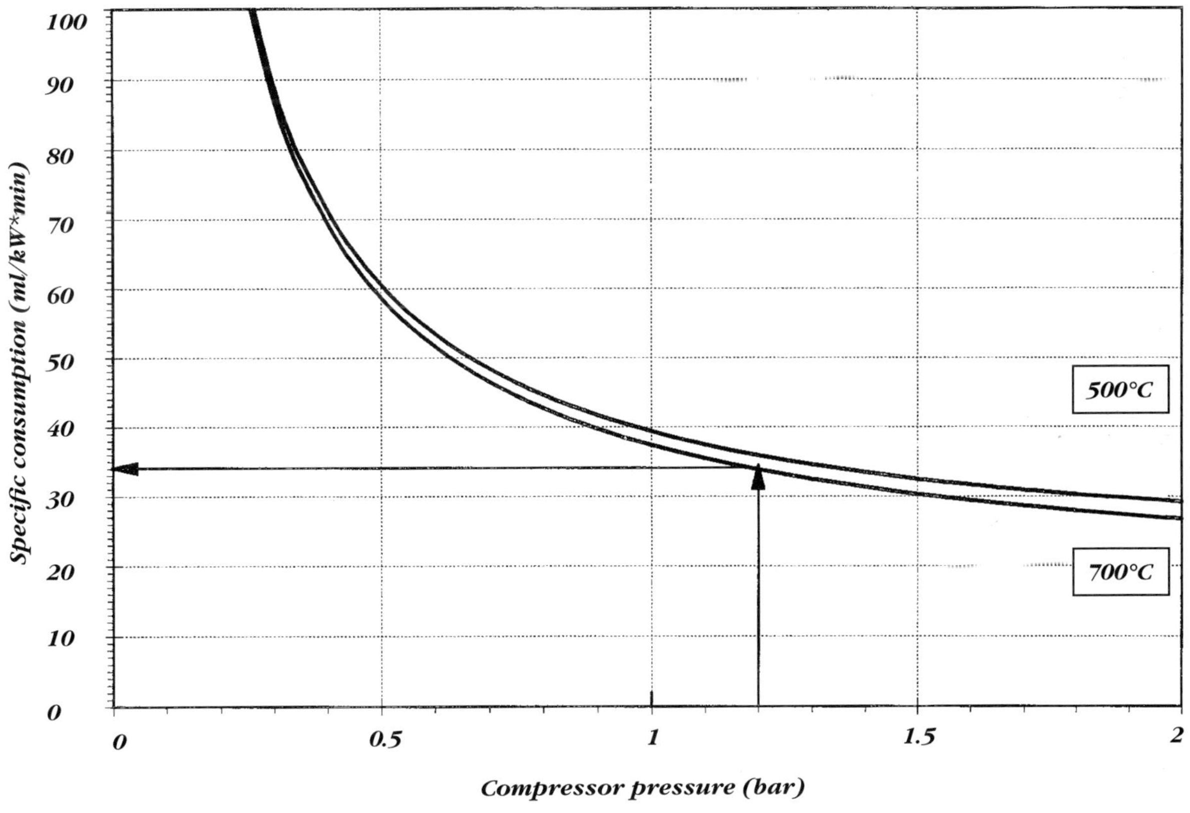

Diagram 9
Specific fuel consumption, varying with compressor pressure and turbine intake temperature.

Turbine engines also work with liquid propane gas, but this fuel calls for a complex high-pressure fuel tank system, and there is the additional problem of carting fairly large propane gas bottles to and fro, with their attendant safety hazards. For these reasons I consider propane gas a poor second choice as a fuel. Admittedly all turbines need a small quantity of propane/butane gas in order to pre-heat the engine, but a supplementary airborne tank is not required for this (see the section entitled "The starting procedure" in the Chapter "Instructions for running the engine").

How much fuel does the engine consume?

It is relatively easy to calculate a turbine's fuel consumption based on its air throughput and exhaust gas temperature. These engines' thermal efficiency is not particularly high due to the relatively low pressure ratios employed. On the other hand the burn efficiency in the combustor is high, i.e. very little unburned fuel escapes in the exhaust gas.

The relationship between specific fuel consumption and compressor pressure is shown in diagram 9. Specific consumption means fuel consumption per unit of work performed. In normal model flying applications flight times are generally stated in minutes, so the fuel consumption is stated here in ml/min at a power of 1 kW. A typical example will clarify the matter:

Shaft power = 3 kW
Compressor pressure = 1.2 bar
Turbine inlet temperature = 700°C
Actual consumption = 3 x 34 ml/min = 102 ml/min

Differences in fuel consumption between a diesel-petrol mixture and kerosene are negligible.

One surprising fact is that the turbine intake temperature has no great influence on the specific fuel consumption, if we assume that the maximum compressor pressure is 2 bar (max. pressure ratio 3), which is a typical figure for our turbine applications. In theory it can be proved that specific fuel consumption can be reduced if the turbine intake temperature is raised, but this only applies where pressure ratios are much higher. That is why full-size turbine engines work at high pressure ratios and at the same time high running temperatures. This high level of efficiency is only achieved by the use of much more complex, multi-stage compressor and turbine stages.

Now let us return to our diagram, and examine the working range of our turbine engines. We can see immediately that specific fuel consumption rises very significantly at low pressure. That is why a large shaft turbine uses more fuel when throttled back (low compressor pressure) than a smaller engine running at higher pressure to achieve the same power. The terms "large" and "small" here refer to high and low air mass flows.

Fuel metering and power control

The power of the core engine, and therefore the available shaft power, are directly dependent on the rate of fuel delivery. Fuel must be metered at a constant rate. Even a very brief interruption in the fuel flow causes the fire in the combustor to be extinguished, and the engine then inevitably stops.

Fuel can be supplied very effectively by means of a small geared pump whose output is governed by a speed controller linked to the radio control system. The maximum pressure produced by the pump should be about 0.5 to 1 bar higher than the maximum pressure of the compressor, i.e. a fuel pump which can supply a minimum pressure of 3 bar is adequate for our purposes.

Lubricating the bearings

The engine's ballraces operate at very high rotational speeds, and at the turbine end of the engine they are also required to run at high temperatures; they must therefore be supplied with a constant flow of lubricant. The front bearings of the power turbine shaft and the propeller shaft bearings are not so highly stressed, and sealed bearings and long-term grease lubrication are adequate. All the other bearings have a much harder life, and a special lubrication system combined with simultaneous cooling is essential. An oil-air lubrication system has proved excellent in practice, and type 2 turbine oil is a suitable lubricant.

More recently turbo-jet engines have been run successfully using a fuel-oil method of lubrication. This involves adding around 5% of turbine oil to the fuel, and a small quantity of this mixture is routed into the cooling airflow of the bearing cooling system under the pressure of the fuel pump. This method of lubrication has worked reliably to date in my latest engine, the OHDIE 7.

Chapter 7

Auxiliary equipment

Fuel tanks, supply lines, shut-off valves, chokes

A 1000 ml plastic fuel tank with a felt clunk pick-up is a good choice for our purpose. Remember that the fuel lines must be made of petrol-resistant material, and must also be able to withstand a pressure of around 5 bar, at least on the pressurised side, i.e. between the pump output and the engine.

I recommend the type of thick-walled hose designed for petrol engines; it has an internal diameter of about 1.5 to 2 mm.

Of course, thin metal tubing can also be used. To produce a pressure-resistant joint between rubber hoses and metal tubing wire can be wound round the junction.

Rubber hose which is absolutely petrol-proof and at the same time capable of withstanding high pressure has not yet been invented, so it is essential to replace the hoses at regular intervals of two or three months. Suppliers of model steam engines and model engineering requirements are a good source of suitable metal fittings and screwed joints, if you wish to produce a high-pressure fuel line with no plastic components at all. If you wish to operate the

The sportsman's approach: OHDIE 7 can be started with the help of an air pump.

engine using the basic system described in the Chapter "Instructions for running the engine" in the section entitled "Before test-running your engine", you will require two manually operated shut-off valves. The usual types designed for model engines have a Teflon seating, and are suitable for this application. The chokes are made from capillary tubing (hypodermic needles) with an internal diameter of 0.5 to 0.6 m and a length of about 60 mm. The resistance to flow in the system can be adjusted by inserting steel rods into the capillary tubes to a greater or lesser depth, according to the resistance required. The diameter of these rods should be about 0.1 mm smaller than the internal diameter of the capillaries. The capillaries have to be connected to the fuel feed hoses, and this is made possible by soldering them into tubes with an outside diameter of 2 to 3 mm, to suit the internal diameter of the fuel lines you are using.

Pump battery, electronics, auxiliary gas, starter

A separate NiCad battery is necessary to supply energy to the fuel pump. The capacity and number of cells has to be selected to suit the motor used in the pump.

If you wish to keep your installation as simple as possible, a small "speed controller" is all you need to provide remote control of the fuel pump and therefore of the engine. The only important point is to check that the controller is actually designed to handle the number of cells in the battery, and the maximum current which is likely to flow. An electronic control system makes for greater convenience, but is not absolutely essential. These units typically include temperature monitoring, a method of regulating compressor pressure, and variable delay times.

You will need a source of auxiliary gas for starting the engine, and this usually takes the form of a small bottle of propane/butane with a release valve, as generally used to start turbines of this type. Gas cartridges designed for soldering torches are a good choice.

For static experiments on the test-stand a mains operated compressor with an air reservoir of around 10 litres works extremely well. It will need to be capable of producing an air pressure of 5 to 6 bar. Of course, you can also use compressed air from a compressed air bottle, but never be tempted to use pure oxygen to blow the engine into life – unless, that is, you wish to see a wonderful firework display as your turbine goes up in flames.

Those modellers who think of their hobby as a sport may also care to consider the use of a powerful hand-operated air pump instead of a compressor or compressed air bottle. It offers two advantages: it never runs out, and your pumping assistant gets some real exercise. The method is tried and tested, but it does call for some interesting athletic gyrations if you have to carry out the whole starting procedure by yourself.

Chapter 8

Measuring equipment and techniques

Measuring compressor and pump pressure

Low-cost analogue pressure gauges with a measurement range of up to 2 bar (2000 hPa) are a good choice for determining compressor pressure, provided that they do not exhibit serious hysteresis, i.e. that the needle registers very low changes in pressure. It is also important that the zero point on the scale should not be suppressed. If this is not the case, it is difficult to adjust the critical idle setting accurately and reliably. You can check whether the instrument is suitably responsive by blowing into it and watching the needle; incidentally, the maximum you can achieve by lung-power is only about 0.2 bar, so if your proposed pressure gauge does not respond to breathing pressure, it is unsuitable for our purpose.

Electronic measuring equipment is available, offering

The first example of OHDIE 7 in its turbo-prop version on the test-stand, showing the gearbox and propeller. Thrust, propeller speed and compressor pressure are monitored. At this stage lubricating oil was still being fed to the bearings from a separate oil tank. The small box in the foreground on the right contains the radio control system and the control electronics for the fuel pump.

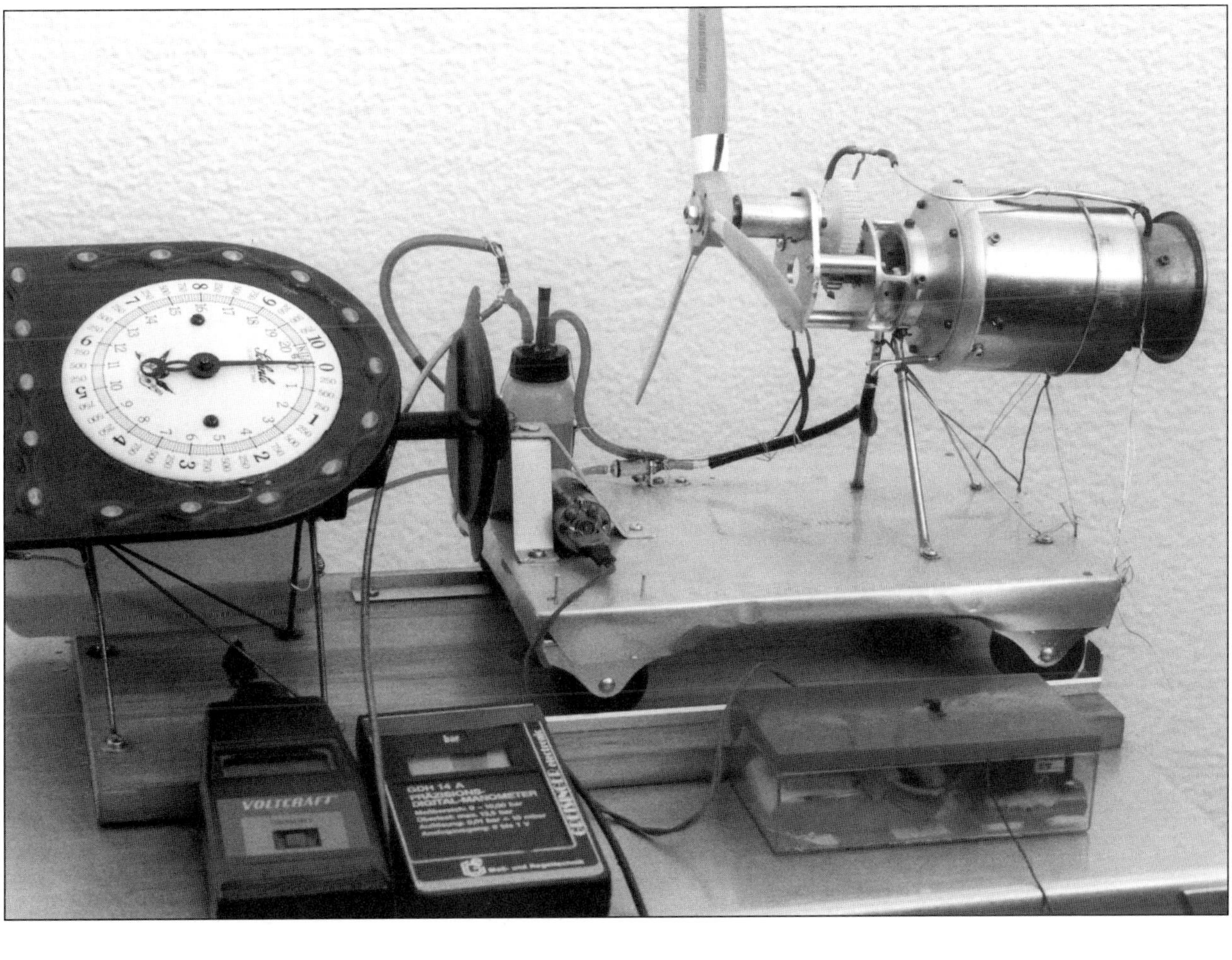

a resolution of 0.01 bar, and these units are also suitable. However, an instrument with a needle is better able to reflect problems in the combustion process; these effects manifest themselves in a marked jittering movement of the needle.

There is one important point on the subject of pressure measurement of which you should be aware: some turbine builders confuse the "pressure ratio", as often quoted in books on the subject, with compressor pressure. In general terms, when we are measuring pressure, we use pressure gauges which register only the excess pressure. For example, if we measure an excess pressure of 1.2 bar, then the pressure ratio (at sea level) can be fairly accurately quoted as 2.2. As we are talking about a ratio between two values of the same type, there is no unit attached to the pressure ratio. If you have a turbine engine of any kind which is designed for a compression ratio of 2.2, and you attempt to run it up to an excess pressure of 2.2 bar, then it is guaranteed to reach the "glowing red all over" stage, if it has not already given up the ghost entirely.

To measure pump pressure you will need a pressure gauge with a measurement range of 5 to 6 bar; in other respects the quality requirements are as already described.

Measuring temperature, rotational speed and thrust

Digital thermometers based on thermo-couples, with a measurement range of up to 1,100°C, are relatively affordable, and an instrument of this type is absolutely essential for measuring the exhaust gas temperature. This value will be about 150°C lower than the turbine intake temperature, but varies according to the load on the turbine. In order to take a measurement the tip of the sensor must be located a few millimetres behind the exit plane of the turbine blades. The temperature distribution is seldom constant all round the periphery, and variations of +/–50°C from the average value can be considered normal. It is therefore important to take measurements at several points in the outlet plane.

To measure the rotational speed of propellers and fans specialist shops can supply contactless rev counters which feature a measurement range suitable for our purpose. The speed of the power turbine shaft can easily be calculated from the gearbox reduction ratio. To measure the rotational speed of the compressor rotor it would be necessary to install a special sensor inside the engine, but in practice this measurement is not really essential. If the exhaust gas temperature stays within the permissible limits, and the compressor pressure is also tolerable, the rotational speed of the compressor can be guaranteed to remain within the safe limits.

If you wish to measure the thrust produced by a fan engine, or when using a fairly small propeller on a turbo-prop engine, you can convert a set of kitchen scales for the purpose: the entire engine is then mounted on a platform running on rollers. This is more difficult if you are using a large propeller in conjunction with an appropriate gearbox, and in this case the recommended route is to measure propeller speed as an indicator of thrust.

Chapter 9

Three shaft turbine engines

With free-running power turbines

OHDIE 5 and the first (turbine-powered) model helicopter

OHDIE 5 was my first practical solution to the task I had set myself of creating a model shaft turbine. There were two crucial reasons for the initial choice of a helicopter:

1. I wanted to be absolutely certain that it was the power turbine stage, driving the main rotor, which was generating the thrust, rather than perhaps the exhaust gas flow. In the case of a helicopter power plant there can be no argument about this.

2. There were commercial factors involved in the professional production of this engine.

As can be seen from the drawing, the actual core engine consists of a turbo-jet engine, modified by the addition of an exhaust gas diffuser.

As the basis for this project I was able to use one of the experimental versions of the FD3/67. The unique aspect of this engine is that the power turbine stage is driven by the intake airflow, i.e. by the air sucked into the core engine. One of the photographs shows the power turbine stage in its dismantled form. The housing is sealed at the front by a plate on which is mounted the shaft tunnel which supports the power turbine. Between the plate and the inner wall of the housing you can see the fixed diffuser vanes, and next to them the power turbine wheel and pinion mounted on its shaft. The housing contains no other moving parts. When the system is assembled, the power turbine wheel is located in front of the diffuser vanes as shown in the diagram. The function of these vanes is to remove any swirl from

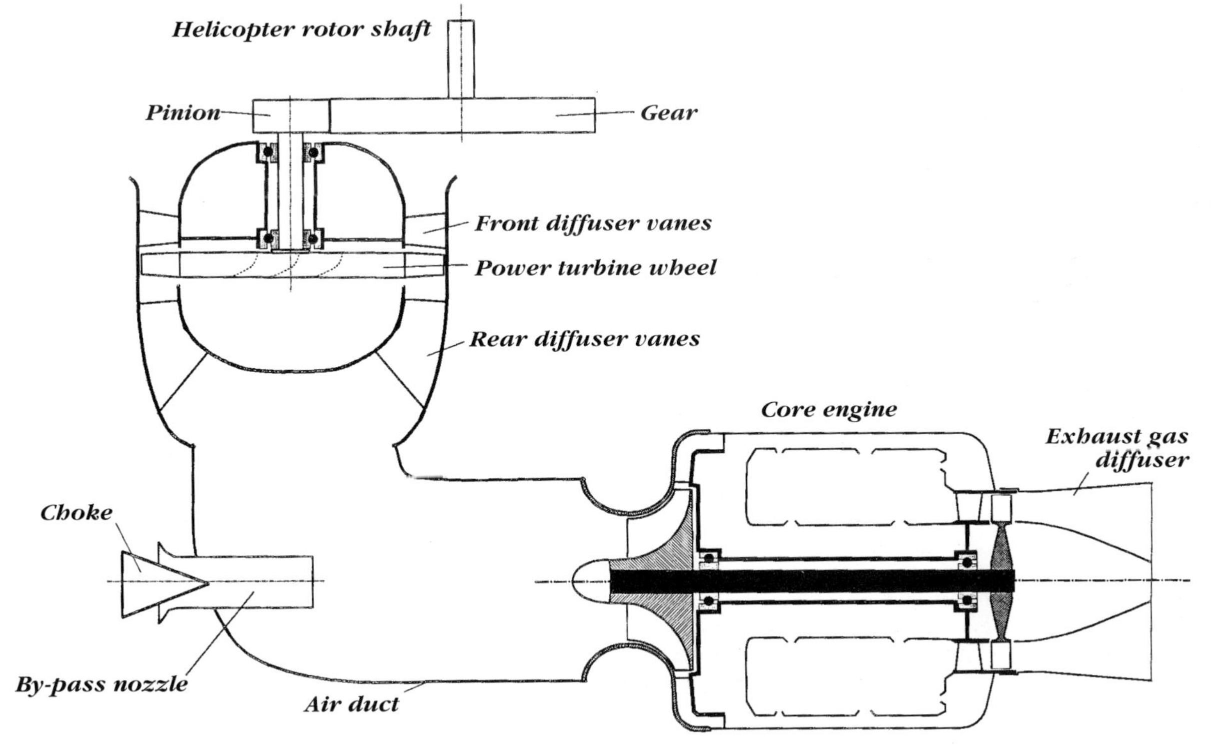

Schematic diagram of OHDIE 5.

The first experimental version of a model shaft power engine with suction turbine. The results led to the building of OHDIE 5.

the airflow as it exits the power turbine stage. This feature was designed to eliminate problems which the primary compressor wheel might have encountered with the turbulent air fed to it.

In a different photo you can see that there is a flexible connection in the form of a hose between the outlet of the power turbine stage and the inlet of the core engine.

When the system is working at its most efficient, the core engine sucks all its air through the power turbine stage. The resultant pressure differential is converted into torque and rotational speed, and thereby into shaft power.

The photograph also shows an additional connection: what is known as the by-pass nozzle. The inlet area of this nozzle is infinitely variable by means of a conical body which acts as a choke. The by-pass nozzle has two functions:

1. It serves as a connection point for the starter fan when starting the engine.

The core engine of OHDIE 5: on the left the exhaust diffuser for operation as a shaft turbine, on the right a thrust nozzle for use as a turbo-jet.

2. When the engine is running, the quantity of air sucked through the power turbine stage can be varied within wide limits by adjusting the conical choke.

   When fully open, shaft power is at a minimum. This places the lowest load on the core engine, which results in a minimum exhaust gas temperature.

The whole system offers the following advantages:

1. The power turbine wheel is located in the cold airflow, and this makes it possible to use a very wide variety of materials for the wheel. The turbine wheel illustrated is made entirely out of plywood, as is the nozzle guide vane system and the housing. In this example the case was reinforced by winding carbon fibre round the outside.

2. There is very little restriction on the diameter of the power turbine wheel, and this factor can then be chosen to determine the optimum rotational speed of the system. The diameter of the wheel shown here is 110 mm, and its rotational speed at a nominal load of around 1,000 W is 15,000 r.p.m. This corresponds approximately to the rotational speed of a 10 cc two-stroke engine. This in turn means that a special gearbox is not required for the model. In the example shown, the only change in the gearing was to the pinion; the original pinion had 13 teeth, but for the

The power turbine wheel, shaft, pinion and housing of OHDIE 5. The housing is made of plywood and is stiffened on the outside with a winding of CFRP. The diffuser vanes can just be seen in the annular opening. The power turbine is made exclusively of plywood.

This picture shows the mounting points on the frame and on the turbine, and also the air duct to the power turbine stage.

turbine-driven model it was replaced by a 10 tooth version. All the other parts of the helicopter mechanics, including the rotor blades, were left unchanged.

3. As there is no mechanical connection of any kind between the power turbine and the core engine, it is possible to control the power output of the core engine without having to worry about the momentary rotational speed of the power turbine shaft. In fact the core engine continues to run undisturbed even if the power turbine shaft is stalled; the only change is a slight rise in the core engine's running temperature.

4. The variable by-pass nozzle can be used to make fine adjustments to the operation of the power turbine stage. If the power turbine restricts the airflow excessively and overloads the core engine, the load on the core engine can be relieved by opening the by-pass nozzle; a feature which is particularly useful in the model helicopter application. With the by-pass nozzle fully open, it proved possible to hold the main rotor stationary even when the core engine was running at full throttle. As a result it proved possible to remove the standard clutch, as required for piston engine power.

5. The orientation and installation of the core engine are not critical, and can be chosen within reasonable limits to suit the model. In virtually any model it would be possible to make up the essential connection between the power turbine and the core engine by fitting an air duct of a suitable shape.

6. The system is not restricted to use with the turbo-jet engine shown here; in fact, any other turbine could be used. The only requirement would be to construct and install a suitable exhaust gas diffuser, and – of course – to produce a power turbine stage designed to match the core engine.

As the photographs prove, this engine has actually flown in a helicopter; the machine's first flight took place on 27th October 1995, and in all probability this was the first successful application of a shaft turbine in a model. The pilot was Uwe Welter, who at that time was a factory colleague of Dieter Schlueter. As the more senior modellers amongst you will probably know, Herr Schlueter was the great pioneer in the field of model helicopters. He assisted us and acted as witness for this first flight.

For model helicopter flyers here are a few technical details relating to this experimental model: the helicopter was an example of the Kalt Baron GS Alpha. Originally it had been fitted with a 22 cc petrol engine and had a rotor diameter of 1.56 m. A detailed report on this experiment was published in the 3/96 issue of FMT (Flug- und Modell-Technik – German model magazine) under the title "Model helicopter with turbine power: world's first". The take-off weight of the helicopter was 5.7 kg, and the rotor speed in flight was measured at 1,050 r.p.m.

View of the first turbine-powered model helicopter from above. The turbine can be seen installed at right-angles to the fuselage centreline, together with the somewhat oversized exhaust gas diffuser.

The two-stroke engine of a model helicopter shown here is replaced by the OHDIE 5 shaft turbine engine.

Naturally, it would be interesting to know the extent to which the principle of the low pressure turbine can be exploited. If we assume an exhaust gas temperature of 600°C as a practical limit, then we can safely run the system at a low pressure of 0.2 bar. In this case the shaft power is 1,000 W. These figures are estimates and based on calculations, but they fit very well with practical experience to date. The weight of the whole engine, i.e. including the power turbine stage and ducting, was 1.5 kg.

This amazingly simple solution is certainly capable of further development, but it does have one essential disadvantage: the greater the pressure differential at the power turbine stage, the smaller the absolute pressure at the intake of the core engine, and this means that the core engine can only operate at a fairly low pressure ratio.

The rules of thermo-dynamics dictate that specific fuel consumption inevitably rises in this situation. The net result is that this arrangement is not such a good choice for a high-power engine where low weight and reasonable fuel consumption are important factors.

The helicopter gearbox consists of the pinion on the power turbine shaft and the original main gear.

OHDIE 6 – the first engine with a "hot" power turbine stage

The next step was to work out a method of persuading a standard turbo-jet engine to surrender a higher proportion of its power than is possible using the intake turbine principle already described. In terms of physics it is fairly simple to prove that such a system must work, so all I had to tackle were the technical problems.

As already discussed in the first chapter, the

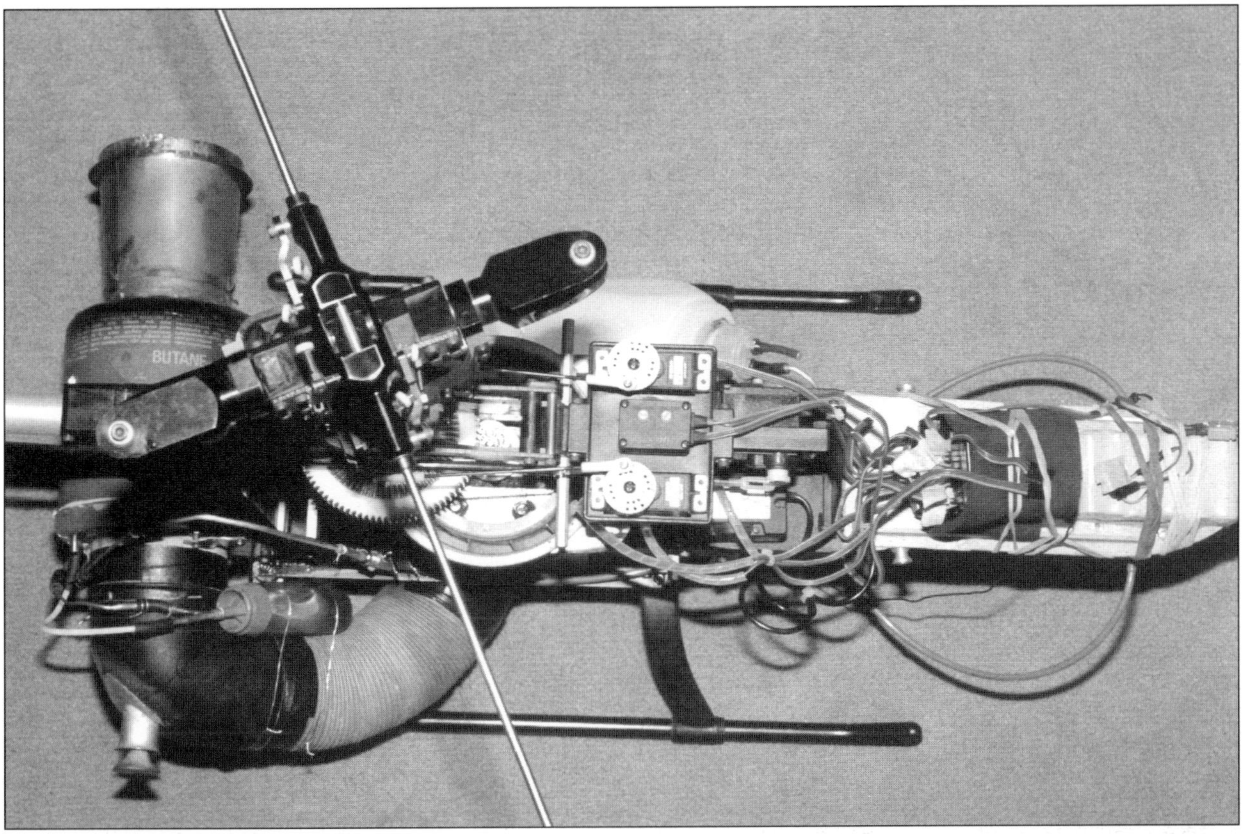

A view into the centre of the helicopter.

Things can get a little warm when starting a turbine.

The first hop!

Photographic proof: the first turbine-powered model helicopter actually flying!

aim would then be to build a relatively small turbine engine whose shaft power would lie in the range 2 to 3 kW.

The first stage was to make a reduced-scale version of a conventional turbo-jet engine of the Thomas Kamps Micro type or KJ-66, and this proved possible and indeed straightforward. The smaller compressor wheel used is also made by KKK, and has a diameter of 50 mm. The shape of this wheel is very similar to those employed in the larger turbo-jet engines mentioned above. Air throughput at the same peripheral speed and maximum efficiency is around 100 g/s. According to the KKK data sheet maximum efficiency is 73%, whereas the company claims a figure of 76% for the larger compressor wheels. The housing is based on a small gas cartridge of 88 mm diameter, and the turbine nozzle guide vanes are welded to this. One of the photos shows the compressor wheel used in the engine, together with the small turbine wheel used with it. The diameter of the turbine wheel was 51 mm. It was made as a one-piece unit from a grade of steel that was reasonably heat-resistant, although not extremely so. This material placed a limit on the engine's power. The engine ran at the first attempt, and produced a thrust of 25 N at a pressure ratio of 1.7. It could only be run up to a rotational speed of 125,000 r.p.m., at which level the compressor generated a pressure of 0.7 bar. Much higher power levels could be expected if an alloy offering greater heat resistance were to be used.

Size comparison of wheels: the compressor wheel and the small turbine wheel are those of the OHDIE 6; below them is a cast blank for the Artes turbine wheel designed for the KJ-66. The large wheel is from a full-size helicopter.

During the Whittle Ohain Trophy event held in Summer 1996 I had the opportunity to discuss at great length the concept of the "hot" power turbine stage with my Spanish friends Dr. Jesus Artes and Matias Duran, based on the principle that the core engine was to be unmodified. The final communiqué which resulted from this discussion was photographed, and is reproduced here – the beermat. The more expert reader will undoubtedly be able to decipher this drawing – at least, if that expert happened to be present at the time of the discussion.

Initial test results were positive, so I then made the effort to produce a simplified cross-sectional drawing of the entire engine which was at least reasonably accurate.

The next step was to develop a suitable power turbine stage. A reduction in axial velocity in the power stage was necessary, and the easiest way of achieving this is to employ a larger turbine wheel. Fortunately I was able to persuade Mr. Artes to part with one of the first professionally cast turbine wheels which he had developed in conjunction with Thomas Kamps. These wheels were actually intended for our KJ-66 jet turbine, but formed an excellent power turbine wheel for the OHDIE 6. The diameter of this wheel is 66 mm.

As can also be seen in the photograph, the power turbine stage consists of two parts which are fitted together. The problem with this arrangement is that the gearbox shaft and gearbox complete with bearings have

The designer and author of this book with OHDIE 6 during the first ever test running session.

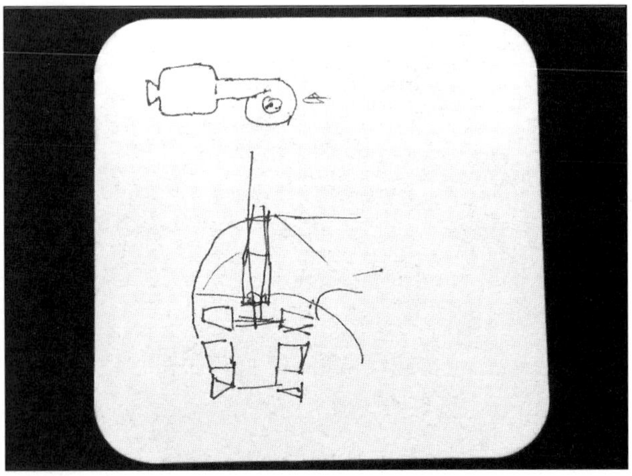

A brain-storming session on the subject of shaft turbine engines produced this sketch on a beer mat. The end-result was called OHDIE 6.

to be protected from the hot exhaust gas flow. This is the solution I came up with:

1. A flow of cooling air and lubricating oil is fed to the actual shaft tunnel which supports the power turbine. As the diagram shows, the cooling air and oil is able to flow through both bearings, and thereby both cools and lubricates them. This arrangement made it possible to make the shaft tunnel from standard aluminium alloy.

2. The shaft tunnel for the power turbine shaft was also enclosed in a second sleeve, which communicated with the power turbine wheel by means of several slots. This allows some of the cooling air to flow round the outside of the shaft tunnel, and in practice this system did lubricate and cool the ballraces adequately.

3. As can be seen in the photographs, the rear of the casing is angled and open to the air, and also features a deflector plate at the gearbox end. This arrangement forces the exhaust gas to flow out and upwards at an angle, as shown in the diagram.

The next problem was how to lubricate the gears, but this one solved itself. A proportion of the air-oil mixture, flowing out of the rear ballrace, happens to strike the gears at the point where they mesh, and this provides more than adequate lubrication. In one of the photographs you can clearly see the globs of oil on the light-coloured table top downstream of the gears.

The gearbox consists of a 15-tooth, modulus 1, brass pinion and an 80-tooth Novotex main gear. This pair of gears made it possible to locate the tunnel for the propeller shaft very close to and parallel with the main engine. Although the main gear is only 3 mm thick, the first signs of wear were actually found on the brass pinion. The tunnel for the propeller shaft consists of a simple aluminium tube, screwed to the compressor housing at the front and to the gearbox block at the rear by means of two lugs. The propeller shaft is a length of 8 mm Ø precision round steel stock.

The starting procedure turned out to be straightforward: I already had a suitable starter fan with adaptor, and this was fitted directly onto the compressor intake. The propeller was then held still while the core

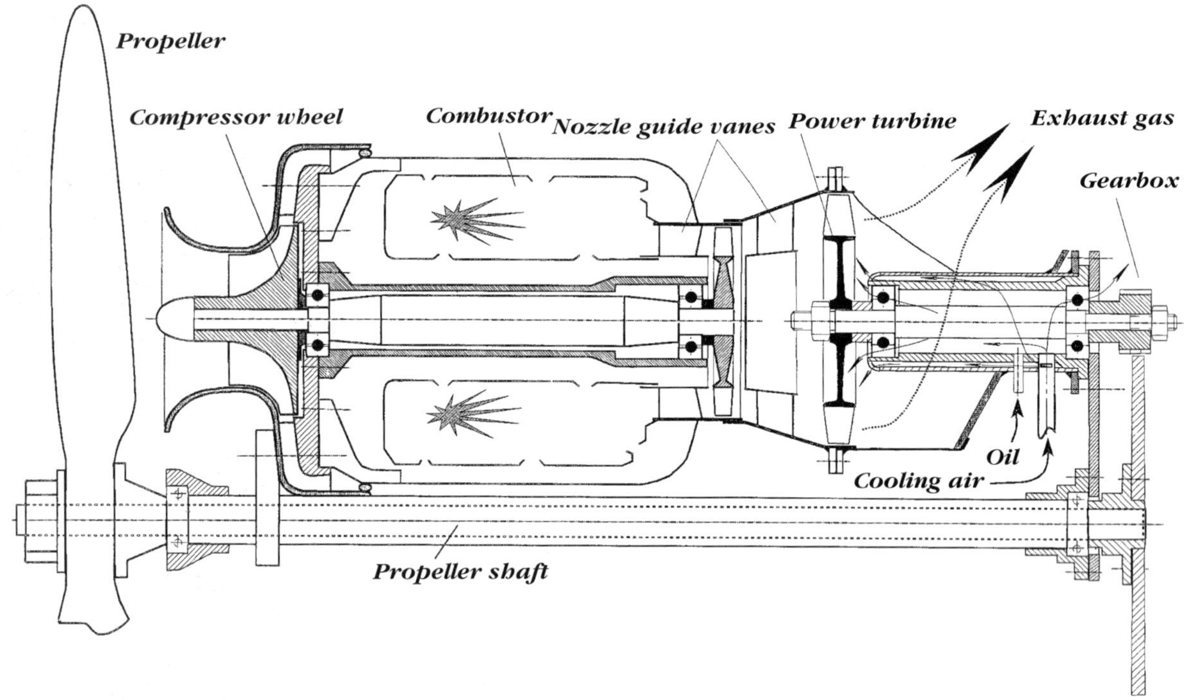

Drawing of OHDIE 6, the first model turbo-prop engine using twin-shaft technology and a "hot" power turbine stage.

engine was run up to speed. Pre-heating was carried out in the usual way using auxiliary gas from a small cartridge. A glowplug was installed on one side of the engine, projecting into the combustor, and this ignited the mixture. It also proved possible to initiate combustion by applying a flame rather carefully from the rear, between the two turbine stages, with the fan running and auxiliary gas supply switched on.

With the engine mounted on the test bench, the next step was to examine its operating characteristics with different sizes of propeller. It turned out that propeller size only has a small influence on the temperature of the exhaust gas. Indeed, the core engine continued to run without problem even when the propeller was held stationary.

The first version of OHDIE 6 capable of running.

The dynamic behaviour of the core engine was very similar to that of a larger turbo-jet, but I was surprised at the dynamic behaviour of the power turbine. A relatively slow rate of acceleration was to be expected, since the core engine could not run up to speed as fast as other power plants such as a good two-stroke motor. However, as exhaust gas temperature automatically rises with increasing engine speed, the work capacity of the power turbine increases at slightly lower pressure. The net result was that throttle response was satisfactory, and adequate for practical flying. The engine was used with a manual power control system based on a standard speed controller and geared fuel pump.

For the initial test-runs the nozzle guide vanes before the power turbine were not fitted, and the engine did run satisfactorily in this state. The most suitable propeller for this version turned out to be a 15" x 12" APC type, which it turned at a maximum speed of 6,500 r.p.m., corresponding to a shaft power of around 800 W. Installing the nozzle guide vanes before the power turbine wheel increased the rotational speed with the same propeller to 8,100 r.p.m., with all other conditions unchanged. This equates to a shaft power of 1,600 W, i.e. double the power. Diagram 10 shows the data calculated from the measured results, corresponding to flying conditions using a compressor pressure of 0.7 bar.

With the maximum power as stated it is possible to calculate the rotational speed of the power turbine wheel based on the gearbox reduction ratio of 5.33:1. The figure was 43,000 r.p.m., which is below the maximum load limit of the power turbine wheel. However, later experiments showed that wheels based on the type used in my first FD 3/64 were also suitable for this arrangement. The next chapter describes their construction.

In late Autumn 1996 everything was ready for the first

View of the power turbine and gearbox of OHDIE 6.

OHDIE 6 on the test-stand. The gearbox reduction ratio was 5.33:1, the rotational speed of the compressor shaft 125,000 r.p.m.

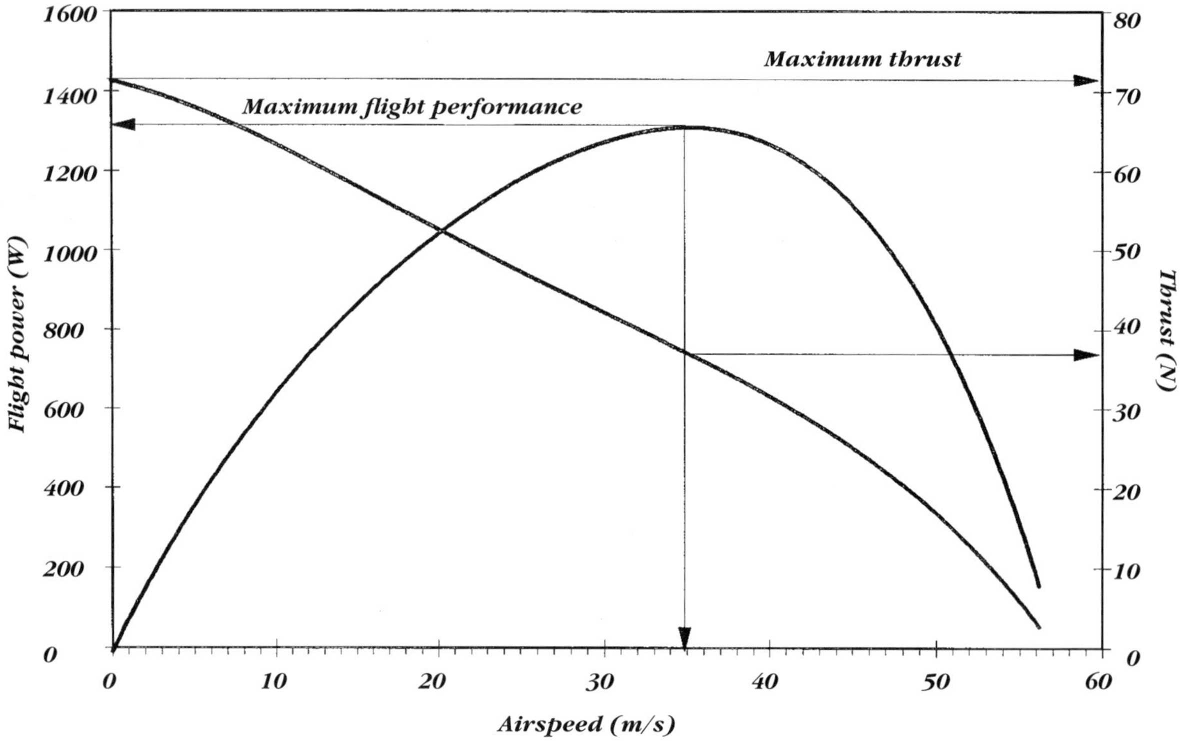

OHDIE 6 shaft turbine engine with 15" x 12" APC propeller

test-flight. The experimental model, complete with engine and 600 ml of fuel, weighed almost exactly 4 kg. In fact a number of take-off attempts had to be aborted before a successful maiden flight was completed. The problem was simply a combination of excess power, a large propeller and a fairly light model. The gyroscopic effect of the large propeller during the take-off run, combined with repeated shocks from the undercarriage, repeatedly resulted in the model running off course. However, cautious handling of the throttle eventually overcome this problem. Once in the air, the model exhibited an extremely impressive performance, to the point that maximum possible power was not used once. Even at a propeller speed of 7,000 r.p.m. the model's speed and rate of climb were outstanding, despite the crude and aerodynamically inefficient installation in the model, as is evident in the photograph.

The 600 ml fuel tank provided plenty of capacity for a ten-minute flight. Compared with a 10 cc two-stroke the fuel consumption is fairly high, but the cost per flight is much lower since kerosene fuel can be used.

After completing these successful experiments I was in two minds about the next step; should I continue the development of this engine, and produce the necessary documentation to allow others to build it, or should I follow up an alternative technical solution which might prove to be more attractive. I decided on the latter.

OHDIE 6 mounted in the experimental aircraft before its first flight in October 1996.

High in the sky: the first fixed-wing model aircraft powered by the OHDIE 6 turbo-prop engine.

Chapter 10

OHDIE 7

The variable engine with concentric shafts

The final section of this book contains the complete building instructions for this engine, but before we get down to business I would like to explain some of the major problems and the solutions I adopted, with reference to the highly simplified drawing below.

1. The shaft of the core engine and the shaft of the power turbine are designed to be concentric, i.e. one rotates inside the other. As the rotational speeds of the two shafts differ widely, their bearing systems must be completely independent of each other, and they must not be allowed to touch at any time. As can be seen from the diagram, the power turbine shaft is necessarily fairly long and thin, and this opens the door to the danger of resonant oscillation at high rotational speed. The shorter and thicker the shaft, and the lower the mass attached to it (e.g. the turbine wheel), the higher the resonant speed.

2. I wanted to use standard commercially produced small compressor wheels. However, the wheel had to be bored out to accommodate the larger tubular shaft, and a different bearing system of correspondingly larger size was required.

3. The bearings for the power turbine shaft must be positioned exactly concentric to the axis of the tubular shaft. The bearing for this shaft at the turbine end of the engine is located virtually in the middle of

Size comparison between OHDIE 7 (left, gearbox removed) and a KJ-66 type turbo-jet.

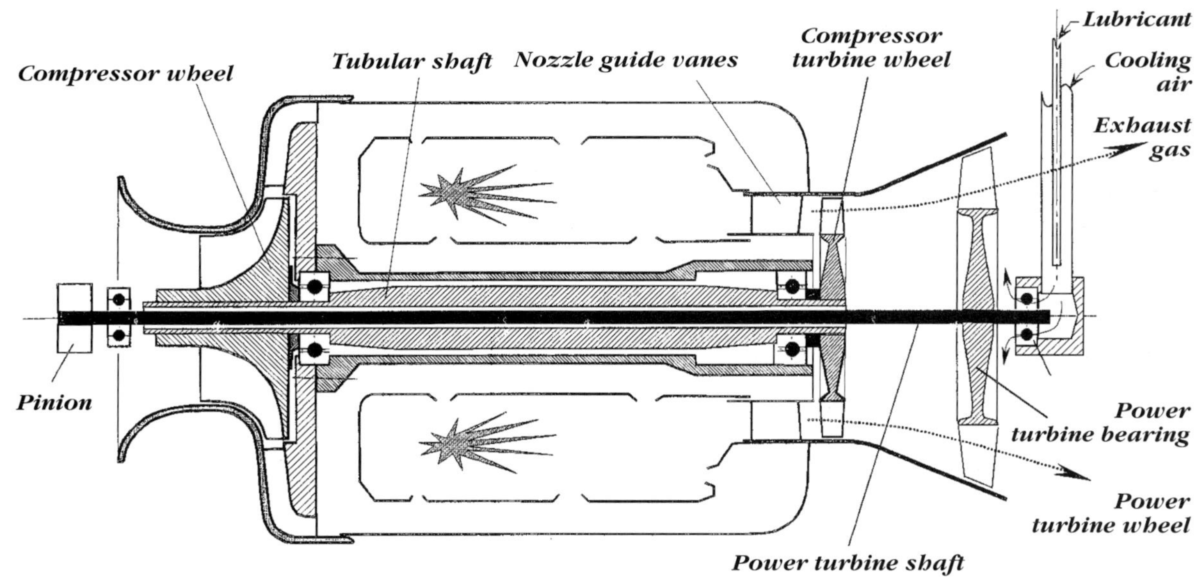

Schematic diagram of OHDIE 7, the first model jet engine with concentric shaft arrangement.

the hot exhaust gas flow, and additional cooling measures are unavoidable.

4. I wanted to spare myself the bother of making a nozzle guide vane system for the power turbine stage, but without accepting a significant power loss. This requirement is met largely by the size of the compressor turbine stage which was selected. Where the gas exits the compressor turbine it still has considerable swirl, or twisting motion, and this makes it possible to eschew a nozzle guide vane system designed to rotate the gas. For further technical details please refer to the next chapter.

Finally, a few words on my experience to date in operating this engine. It was initially subjected to a thorough series of static test runs on the test stand, using various sizes of propeller. The propeller data and measured rotational speeds make it possible to calculate the approx imate shaft power of the engine. When compared with the calculated shaft power of the engine under varying conditions, the results were found to match the estimates very closely.

For the first turbofan version a 2:1 reduction gearbox was used, based on relatively small helical-cut metal gears. The 125 mm Ø fan was taken from a commercially produced impeller system, and the performance was indeed as expected, although the rate of wear in the gearbox was so rapid that I decided to try an alternative solution using a directly driven fan. Instead of having to develop a suitable gearbox, I now had to produce a suitable fan. From the outset it was clear that it could not be made to provide an optimum match for the rotational speed of the power turbine stage, and this compromise was deemed unavoidable and acceptable.

First attempts with the non-geared turbo-fan version betrayed the effects of resonance, producing oscillations in the power turbine shaft. In this case the original seven-bladed fan was mounted directly on the shaft.

Experiments with a turbo-fan and gearbox. The fan wheel is from a standard commercial ducted fan unit, and is driven by a reduction gearbox in this version. The experimental set up shown here already delivered 25 N thrust, without any form of fan duct.

For the ungeared turbofan version of the engine, I made the requisite calculations, built the fan and carried out initial tests. This first shot turned out to be a bull's eye. Diagram 11 shows the results of a series of measurements using this fan. A static thrust of 35 N at a compressor pressure of 0.7 bar gives a good idea of what can be expected. If a compressor turbine wheel were to be made of highly heat-resistant material, the expected thrust should be close to 60 N at a compressor pressure of 1.2 bar.

OHDIE 7 with turbo-fan fitted, still without its jacket. There is a flexible coupling between the power turbine shaft and the fan shaft. In this version of the engine a reduction gearbox is not necessary.

Flight testing

My basic rule is not to present a new engine to the public until it has successfully powered a model aircraft in flight, and both engine and model have landed safely. I have remained true to this philosophy, and this stage was reached in early February 1999.

The experimental aircraft was a Kangaroo, which was originally designed to act as a turbo-jet trainer. Its docile flying characteristics have been widely acknowledged, and together with its large wing area and good visibility the model proved to be an excellent test-bed for the OHDIE 7. Since the engine is mounted above the

This picture of the dismantled fan stage of OHDIE 7 shows the power shaft and claw coupling at bottom left, together with the fan shaft.

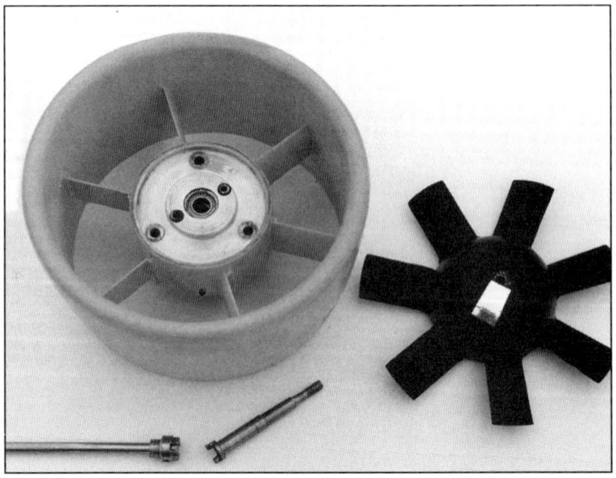

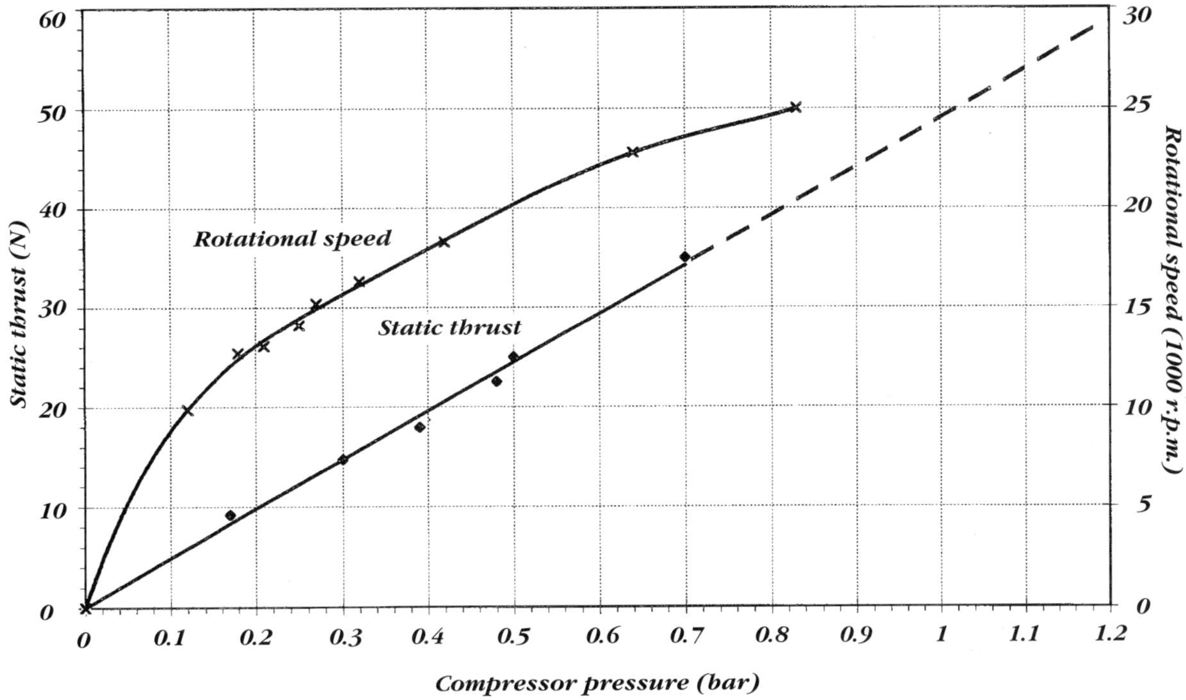

Diagram 11
Measured results of turbo-fan version with OHDIE 7.

fuselage, I designed the gearbox to suit a propeller of relatively small diameter. In view of the propeller manufacturer's stated maximum load, the maximum power of the turbo-prop engine was limited when the model was flown with the new engine; compressor pressure was restricted to a maximum of 0.5 bar for these test-flights, which gave a take-off propeller speed of around 12,000 r.p.m. At this speed the engine

Turbo-fan version OHDIE 7 mounted on a Kangaroo before the maiden flight in March 1999.

The model takes off into a new realm of turbo-fan flying.

OHDIE 7 powering a 6 kg Kangaroo into the sky.

Here I present my latest hardware on the model flying site at RC Palma de Mallorca.

developed a static thrust of 30 N, which was adequate for a safe take-off. In flight there proved to be wide differences between propellers used, i.e. between the three-bladed and two-bladed types. The three-bladed propeller restricted the model to fairly modest airspeeds. The rotational speed of the two-bladed propeller was significantly higher, and this is evident to the ear.

The model's airspeed in level flight was sufficient for relaxed rolls and loops, but elevator correction was found to be necessary every time the engine load was changed. When the throttle was opened, the model showed a clear tendency to dive. When throttled back, the nose tended to rise. However, these pitch trim changes were easily corrected without the need for large control surface movements. One important point to note with this model is the CG position: on no account fly the Kangaroo with the CG further aft than the location stated by the manufacturer; if you do, the model has a distinct tendency to flip onto its back during a slow landing approach – as I discovered to my cost.

When fitted with the non-geared turbo-fan version of the engine, the model's flying characteristics were quite different. The take-off roll was somewhat longer, but in the air this power system produced a substantially higher airspeed; indeed it was reminiscent of the much more powerful turbo-jet engine.

A further satisfying point was the engine's fuel consumption: 1 litre of kerosene or similar fuel gave a flight time of ten minutes. Once the turbine wheels and propeller (or fan) had been dynamically balanced with some care, the engine's noise level was also pleasantly low.

Chapter 11

Building instruction

The OHDIE 7 shaft turbine engine

Introduction

First read, then build! These instructions are aimed at modellers with a solid background and plenty of experience in metal-working. If you have never attempted silver-soldering, and never knew that a "clock" was an essential piece of workshop equipment when processing metal, rather than just a time-piece, then you would be well advised to entrust the work described in these instructions to a model engineer with plenty of experience in the field. You will need a certain amount of machine-shop equipment as an absolute minimum: you cannot build the engine without a lathe and a MIG welder. Specialised tools are also required, and they are listed in the appropriate sections. A milling machine is not absolutely essential, but it certainly makes life easier. I constructed the prototype described here without the help of such a machine, and some of the components are designed to avoid the need for its services.

The parts list states the exact materials recommended, but it is not mandatory to keep strictly to them. In many cases similar materials can be used; for example, materials of similar, but not identical, thickness.

The following notes are intended to help you find your way around the plans: the drawings take up a total of 15 A4 sheets, marked "Sheet 1" to "Sheet 15". The parts list is sub-divided to show the part numbers for the components of each sub-assembly, e.g. parts 9 to 9.11 go to make up the combustor. The sheet which carries the dimensioned drawings for each sub-assembly is stated in the parts list in the column "Sheet No.". The general arrangement drawing on sheet 1 shows all the components. In the text I refer to the parts by description and part number, e.g. "spacer ring 4.6". The note "front view" means in the direction of the airflow. In the general arrangement drawing on sheet 1 this means "looking from left to right". This is important for some of the components, as not all of them are symmetrical.

Dimensioned drawings are not provided for the ballraces, screws and nuts used in the engine. Unless otherwise stated the drawings are shown full-size.

Building the OHDIE 7 engine for commercial gain is not permitted. The design is legally protected under Patent No. 29912110.0.

The drawings and texts have been prepared to the best of my knowledge, but I cannot guarantee that they are error-free, and I deny all liability for compensation due to errors in the information provided.

Chapter 12

Parts list and drawings

Parts List

Part No.	Description	No off.	Sheet No.	Material, blank, initial dimensions, notes
1	Engine housing	1	2	Stainless steel container, 90-100 Ø, wall thickness approx. 0.4
1.1	Pressure meter nipple	1	2	Brass tube, 2 x 0.5 or similar
2	Front cover	1	6	Heavy-duty light alloy, 40 Ø
2.1	Screw	5	1	M3 x 12 cheesehead, socket-head
3	Compressor wheel	1	1	K14-2067GGA S. No. 53141232003 mod. manufacturer: KKK
4	Tubular shaft	1	3	Non-alloyed or low-alloy tool steel, 15 Ø
4.1	Special nut	1	15	M8 x 0.75, left-hand, nickel-chrome steel
4.2	Sealing ring	1	15	Brass, 8 Ø
4.3	Spacer disc	1	15	Precision round steel rod, 25 Ø, silver steel
4.4	Ballrace	1	1	Hybrid spindle bearing, uncaged, ceramic balls, manufacturer: GRW
4.5	Ballrace	1	1	Hybrid spindle bearing, uncaged, ceramic balls, manufacturer: GRW
4.6	Spacer ring	1	15	Nickel-chrome steel, 12 Ø
4.7	Compressor turbine wheel	1	8	Extreme heat-resistant nickel-based alloy, NIMONIC 90 or similar
4.8	Special nut	1	1	As part 4.1
5	Shaft tunnel	1	3 + 15	Heavy-duty light alloy, 40 Ø
5.1	Screw	4	15	M3 x 10 countersunk, socket-head
5.2	Thrust spring	1	15	Spring steel rod, 2 Ø
5.3	Sliding sleeve	1	15	Precision round steel rod, 25 Ø, silver steel
5.4	Lubricant tube	1	2 + 15	Brass tube, 2 x 0.5 or similar
5.5	Feed capillary	1	2 + 15	0.5-0.6 I.D. nickel-chrome steel, syringe needle
6	Power turbine shaft	1	3	Precision round steel rod, 5 Ø, silver steel
6.1	Connecting piece	1	4	Light alloy, 60 Ø
6.2	Bearing housing	1	13	Light alloy, 25 Ø
6.3	Screw	4	1	M2.5 x 8, cheesehead, socket-head
6.4	Ballrace	1	1	5 I.D., 11 O.D.
6.5	Hub	1	15	Precision round steel rod, 12 Ø, silver steel
6.6	Power turbine wheel	1	8	Nickel-chrome steel sheet, 3 thick
6.7	Ballrace	1	1	4 I.D., 9 O.D., no seals
6.8	Bearing housing	1	15	Precision round steel rod, 12 Ø, silver steel
6.9	Strut	2	2	Nickel-chrome steel sheet, 1 thick
6.10	Combination strut	1	2	Nickel-chrome steel rod, 4 Ø
6.11	Clip	1	2	Nickel-chrome steel sheet, 0.5 thick
6.12	Screw + nut	3	1	M3 x 5 cheesehead, socket-head
6.13	Connecting piece	5	2	Brass, 6 Ø
6.14	Tube	1	2	Brass, 5 Ø
6.15	Cooling air tube	1	2	Brass tube, 4 x 0.5
6.16	Capillary	1	2	0.5-0.6 I.D. nickel-chrome steel, syringe needle
6.17	Lubricant tube	1	2	Brass tube, 2 x 0.5, or similar

6.18	Bored lug	3	2	Nickel-chrome steel sheet, 1 thick
6.19	Round-head rivet	1	1	Copper, 3 Ø
7	Diffuser vane holder	1	5 + 15	Light alloy sheet, 3 thick
7.1	Baseplate	1	5 + 15	Light alloy sheet, 3 thick
7.2	Compressor guide vane	15	5 + 15	Light alloy sheet, 3 thick
7.3	Angle bracket	5	5 + 15	Heavy-duty light alloy, 10 x 10
7.4	Screw	10	15	M3 x 5 cheesehead socket-head
7.5	Screw	5	5 + 15	M3 x 10 cheesehead socket-head
7.6	Screw	1	1	M2.5 x 20 cheesehead socket-head
8	Turbine wheel housing	1	7 + 14	Nickel-chrome steel, 70 Ø
8.1	Nozzle guide vane	15	7 + 14	Nickel-chrome-silicon steel sheet, heat-resistant, 0.6 thick
8.2	Inner ring	1	7 + 14	Nickel-chrome steel, 50 Ø
8.3	Starting air nozzle	1	7	Nickel-chrome steel tube, 3 x 0.5
9	Front panel	1	9 + 12	Nickel-chrome steel sheet, 0.5 or 0.4 thick
9.1	Bracket	2	12	Nickel-chrome steel sheet, 0.5 or 0.4 thick
9.2	Threaded bush	2	12	Nickel-chrome steel, 6 Ø
9.3	Screw	2	1	M3 x 5 cheesehead, socket-head
9.4	Outer wall	1	11 + 12	Nickel-chrome steel sheet, 0.5 or 0.4 thick
9.5	Inner wall	1	10 + 12	Nickel-chrome steel sheet, 0.5 or 0.4 thick
9.6	Stick	6	11 + 12	Nickel-chrome steel tube, 5 x 0.5
9.7	Back panel	1	9 + 12	Nickel-chrome steel sheet, 0.5 or 0.4 thick
9.8	Annular tube	1	12	Brass tube, 3 x 0.5, or similar
9.9	Bracket	3	12	Nickel-chrome steel sheet, 0.5 or 0.4 thick
9.10	Feed capillary	6	12	0.5-0.6 I.D. nickel-chrome steel, syringe needle
9.11	Auxiliary gas feed tube	1	12	Brass tube, 2 x 0.5, or similar
9.12	Fuel feed tube	1	12	Brass tube, 2 x 0.5, or similar
10	Pinion	1	1	Brass, 15-tooth, modulus 1, tooth width 8, with hub
10.1	Grubscrew	1	1	M3 x 5, socket-head
10.2	Gear	1	1	Plastic, 35-tooth, modulus 1, tooth width 8, with hub
10.3	Screw + nut	1	1	M3 x 20 cheesehead, socket-head
10.4	Propeller shaft	1	13	Precision round steel rod, 12 Ø, silver steel
10.5	Ballrace	2	1	6 I.D., 19 O.D., width 6, lubricated for life
10.6	Bearing housing	1	13	Light alloy, 40 Ø
10.7	Spacer sleeve	1	13	Light alloy, 12 Ø
10.8	Plate	1	13	Light alloy sheet, 3 thick
10.9	Screw	4	1	M3 x 8
10.10	Spacer sleeve	3	13	Light alloy, 10 Ø
10.11	Screw	3	1	M4 x 40, cheesehead, socket-head
10.12	Spacer sleeve	1	13	Light alloy, 8 Ø
10.13	Spacer washer	1	13	Light alloy, 25 Ø
11	Alignment body A	1	14	Light alloy, 70 Ø
11.1	Alignment body B	1	14	Precision round steel, 12 Ø, silver steel
11.2	Screw	1	14	M3 x 15, cheesehead, socket-head
11.3	Mandrel	1	11	Steel, 12 Ø
11.4	Punch	1	11	Steel, 12 Ø

Dimensioned drawings, sheets 1 to 15

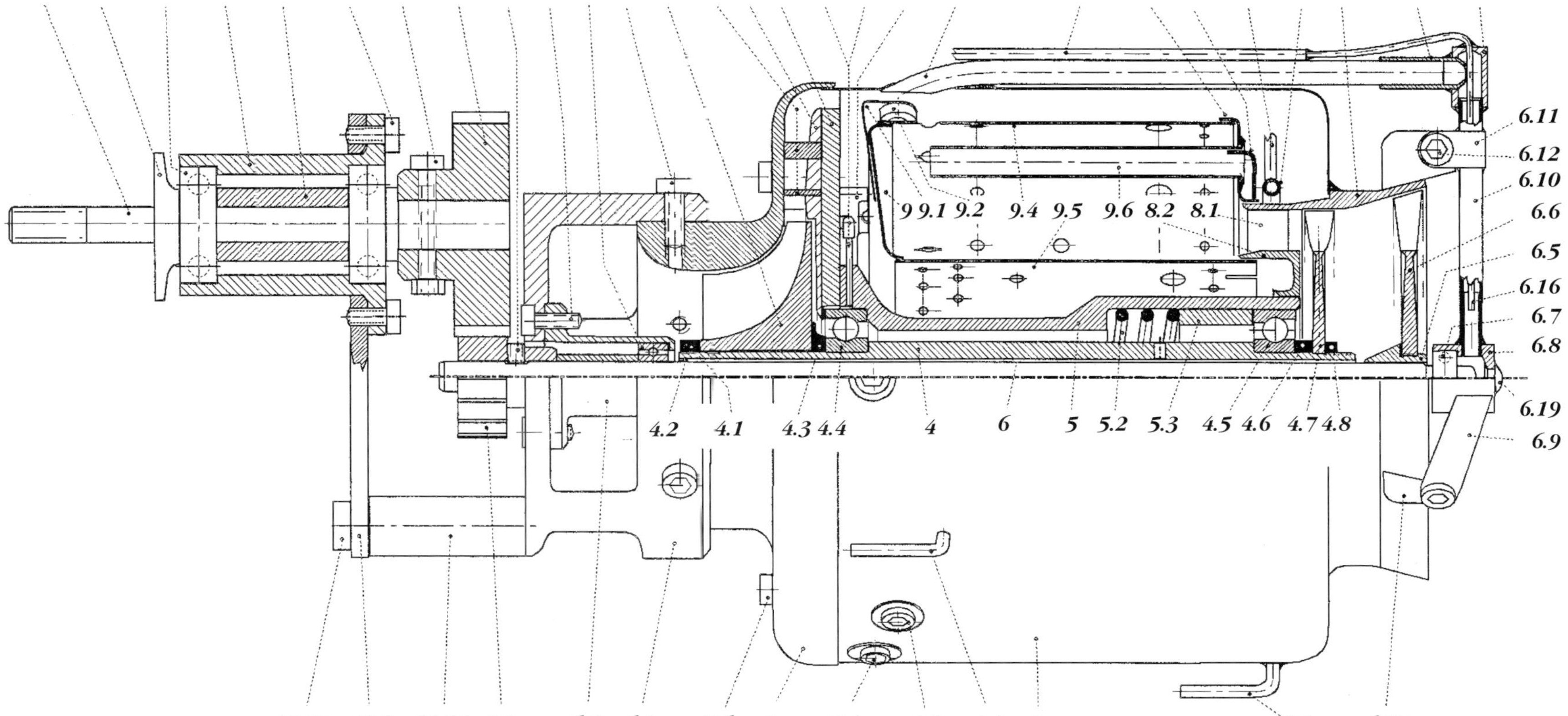

Sheet 1 of the drawings for the OHDIE 7 shaft power engine.

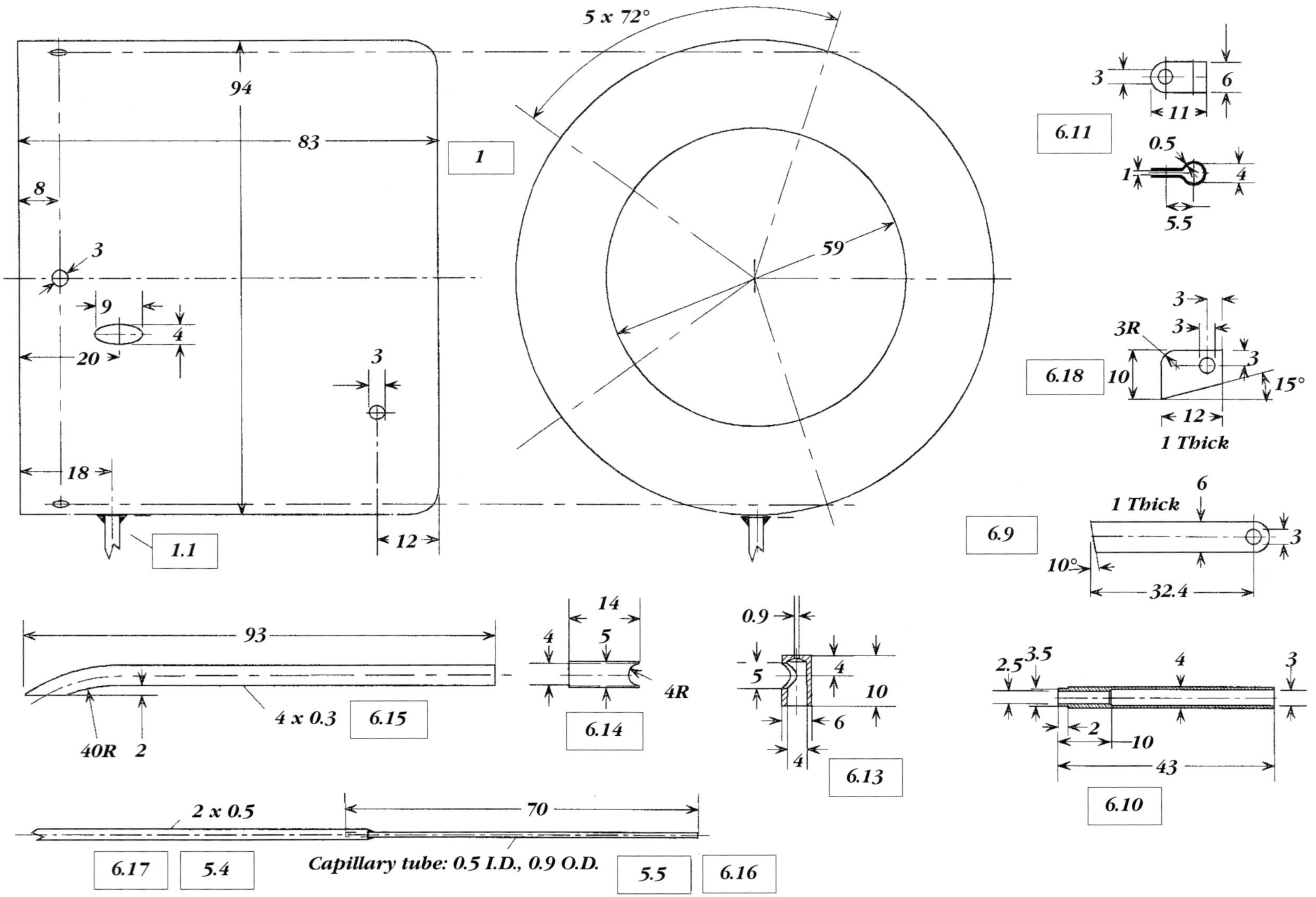

Sheet 2 of the drawings for the OHDIE 7 shaft power engine.

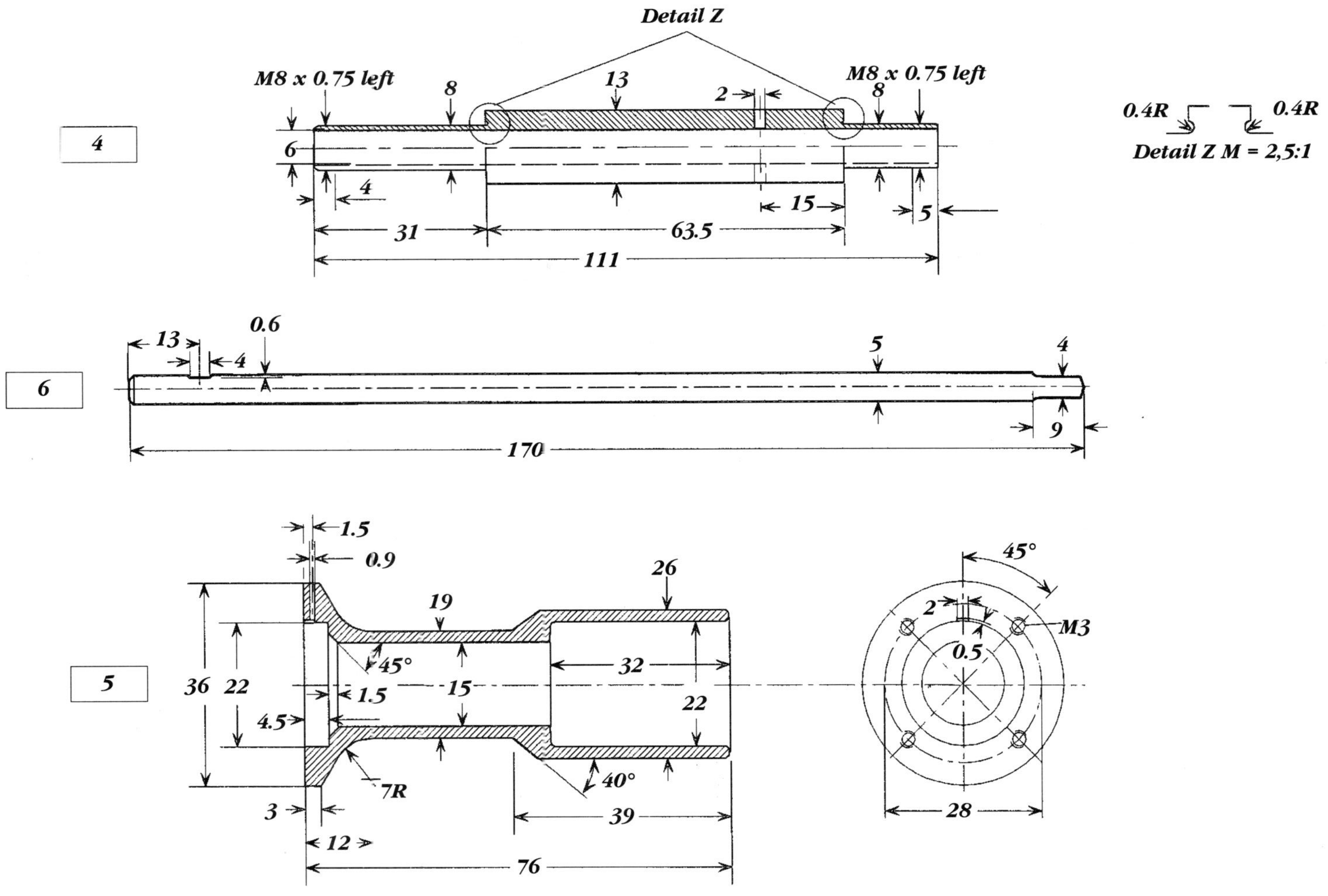

Sheet 3 of the drawings for the OHDIE 7 shaft power engine.

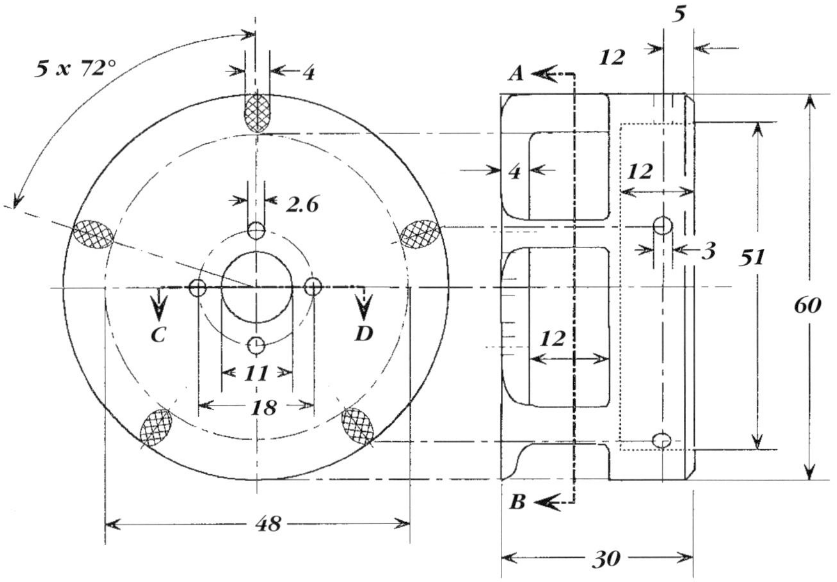

6.1

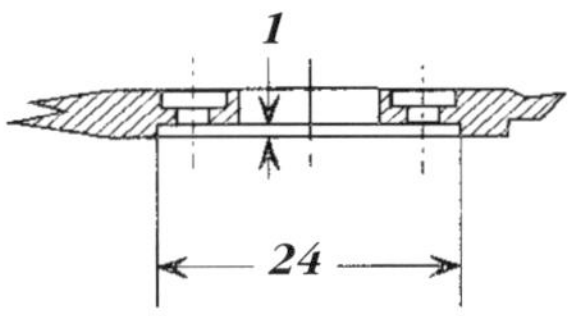

Section C-D

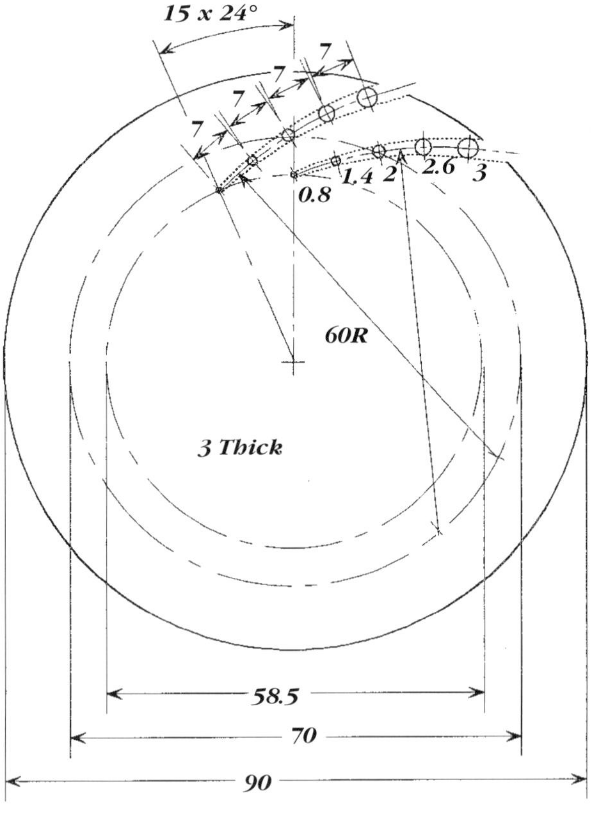

Preparation 7
View from front

Sheet 4 of the drawings for the OHDIE 7 shaft power engine.

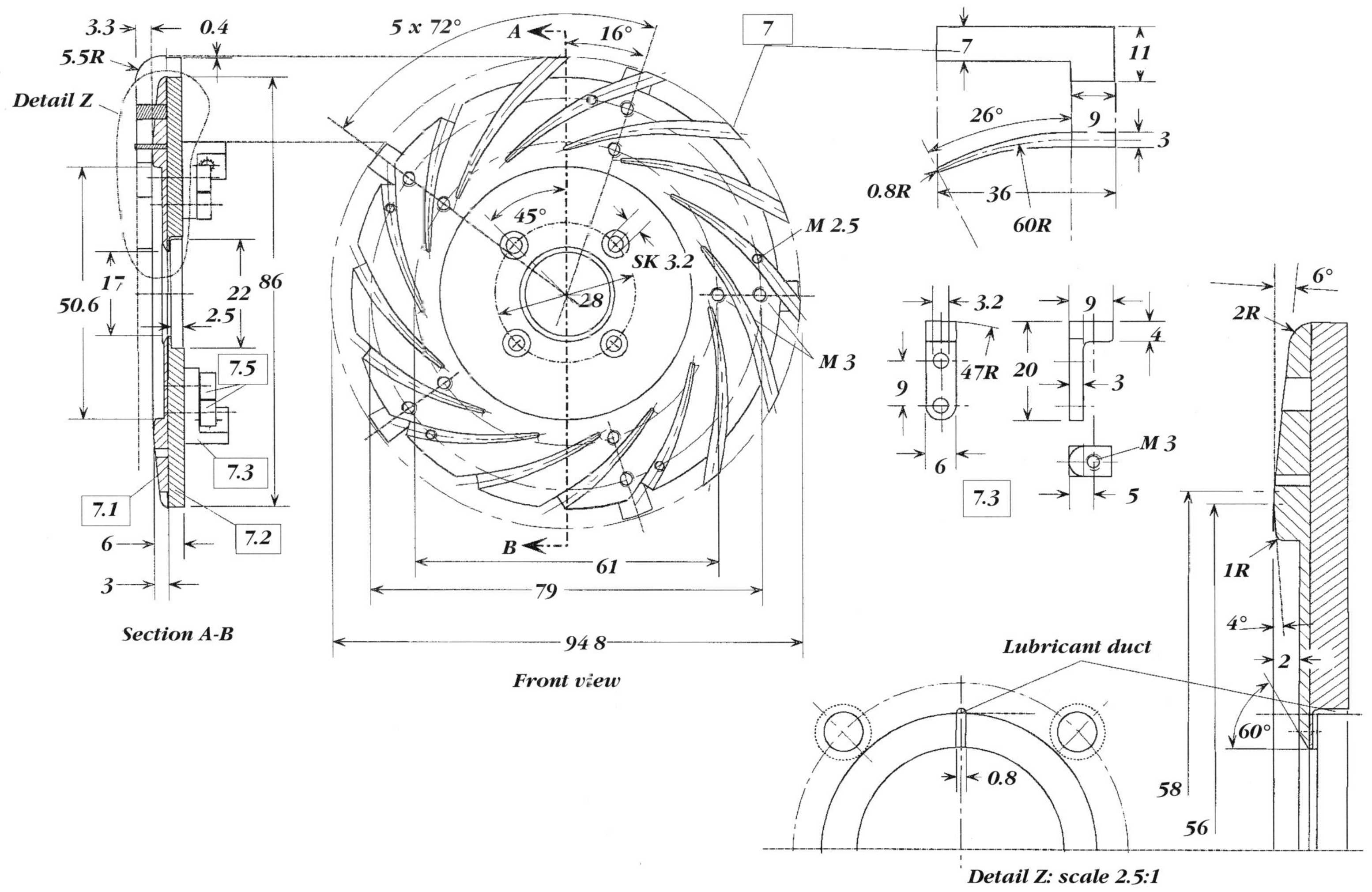

Sheet 5 of the drawings for the OHDIE 7 shaft power engine.

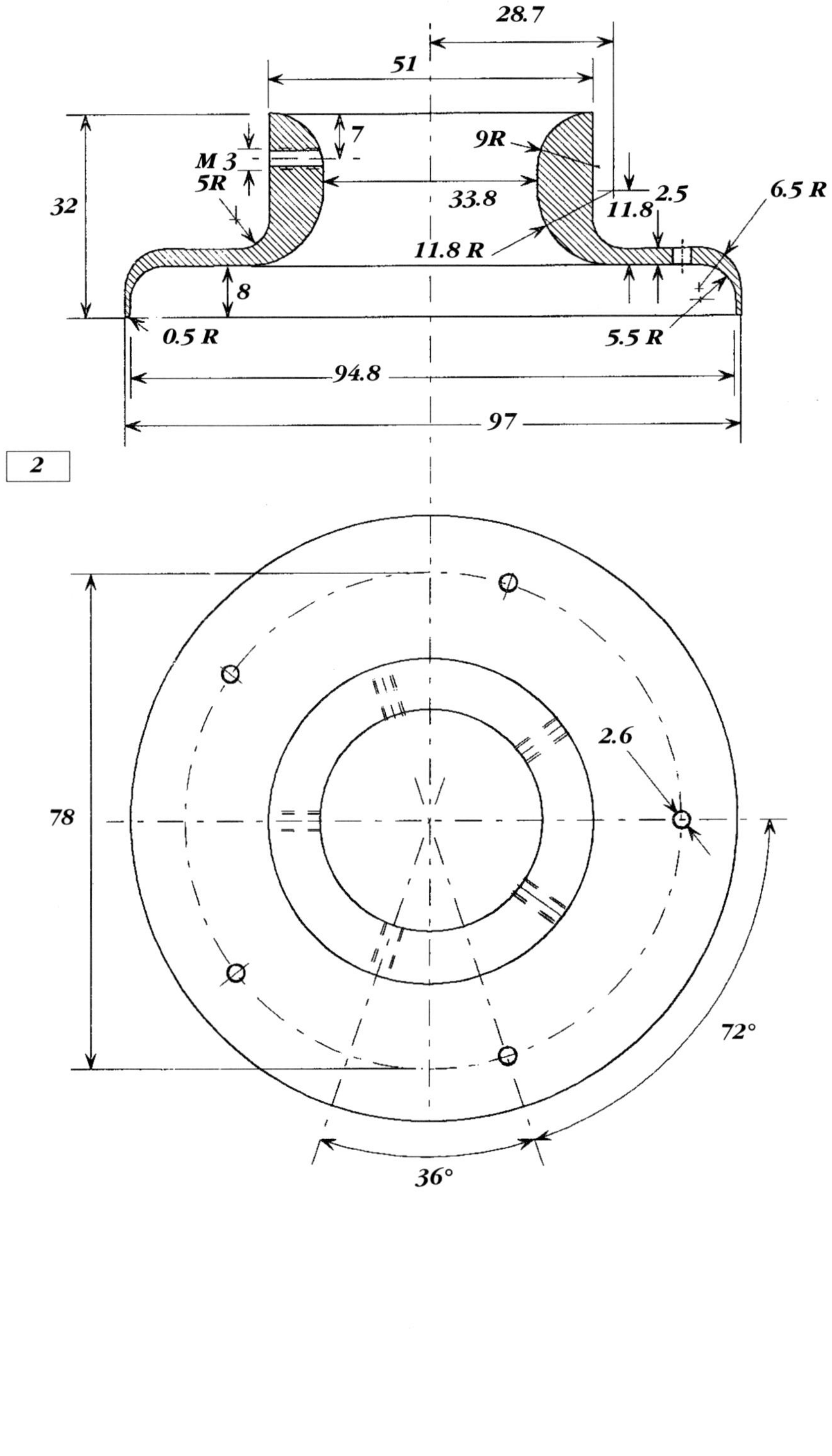

Sheet 6 of the drawings for the OHDIE 7 shaft power engine.

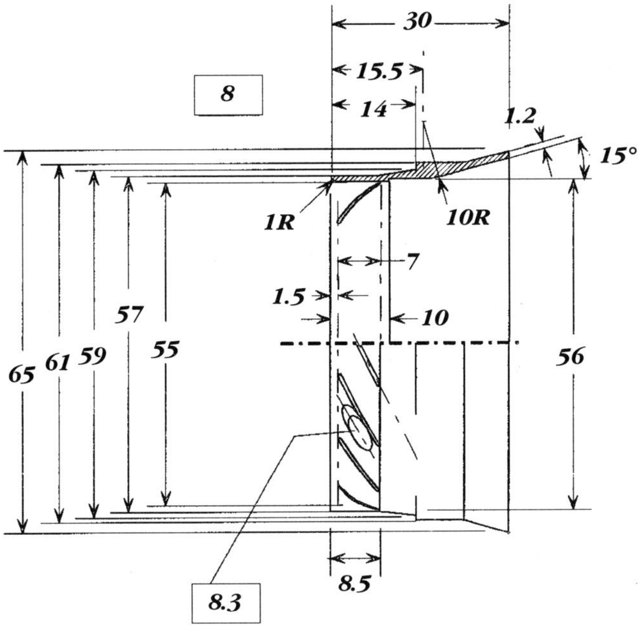

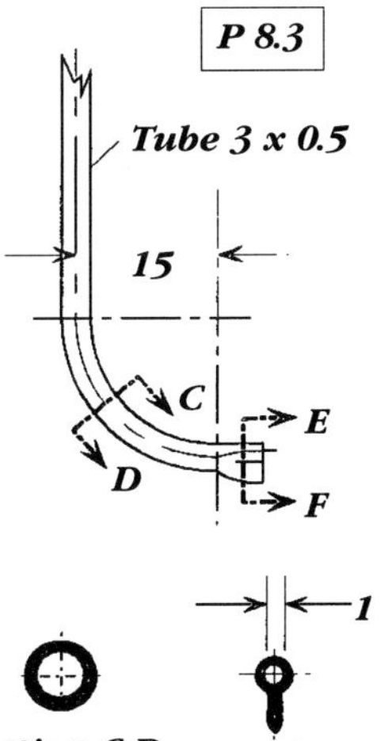

Section C-D
Scale 2.5:1

E-F

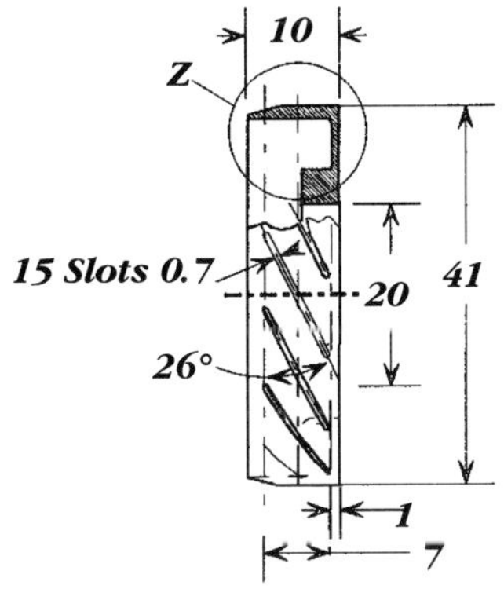

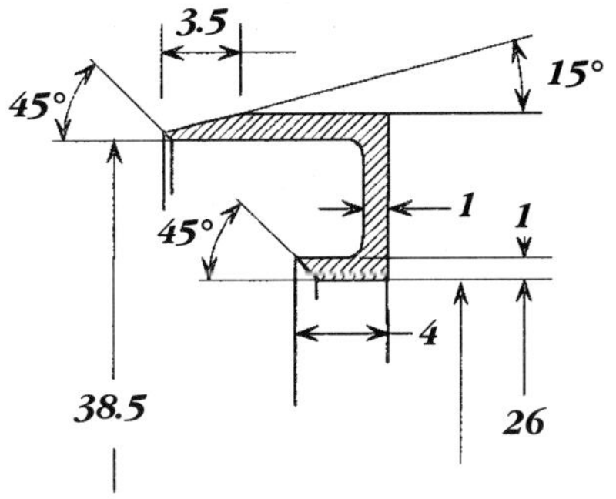

8.2 Before joining 8.1 and 8.2

Detail Z, finished dimensions
Scale 2.5:1

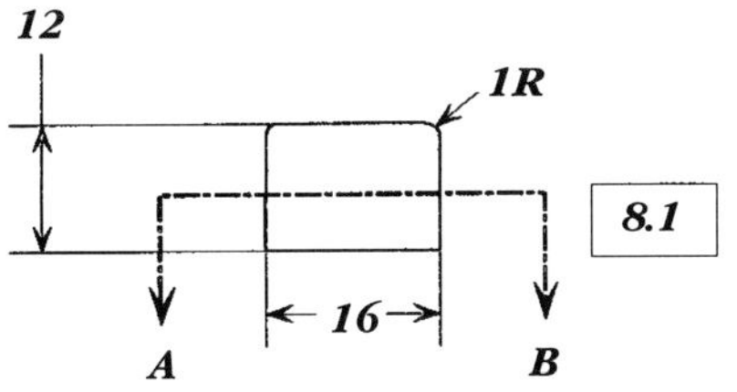

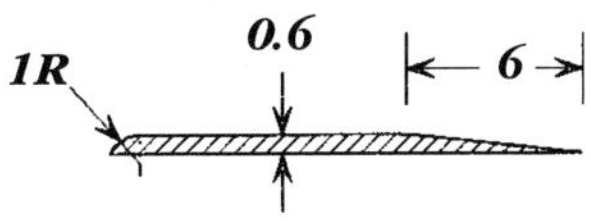

Section A-B
Scale 2.5:1

Sheet 7 of the drawings for the OHDIE 7 shaft power engine.

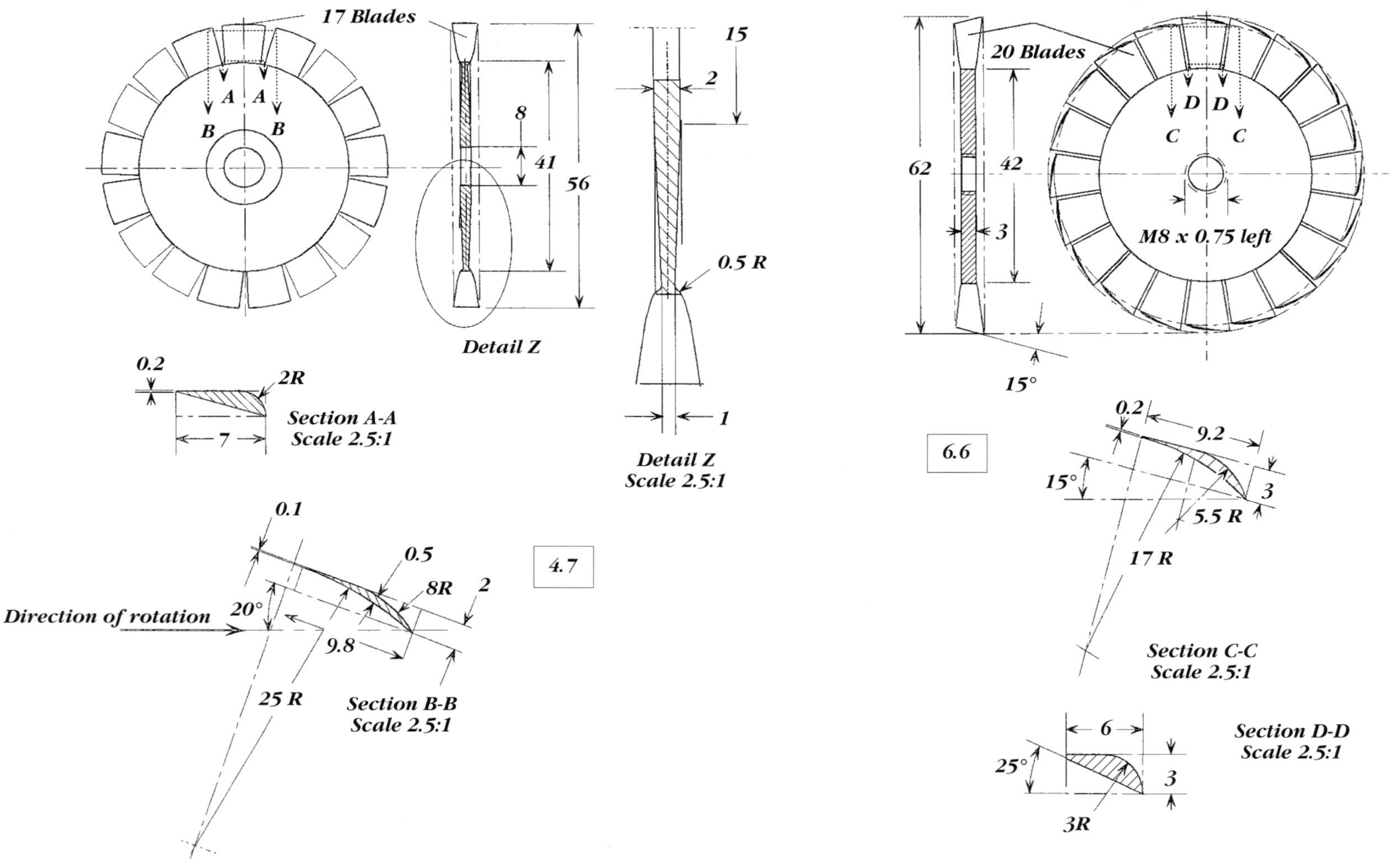

Sheet 8 of the drawings for the OHDIE 7 shaft power engine.

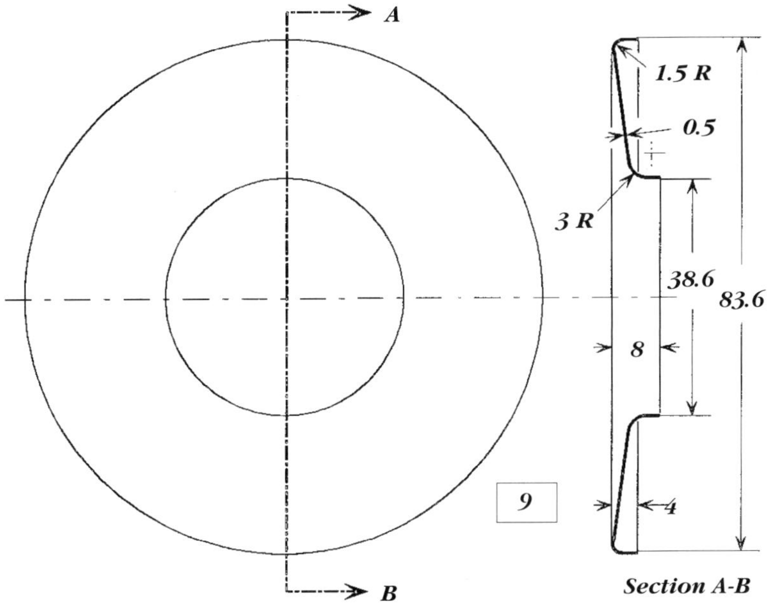

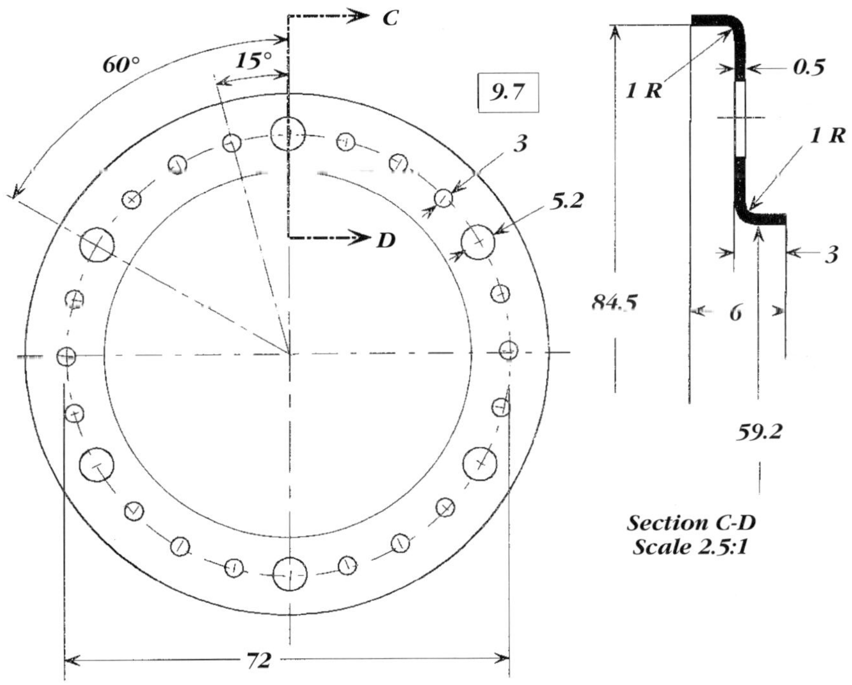

Sheet 9 of the drawings for the OHDIE 7 shaft power engine.

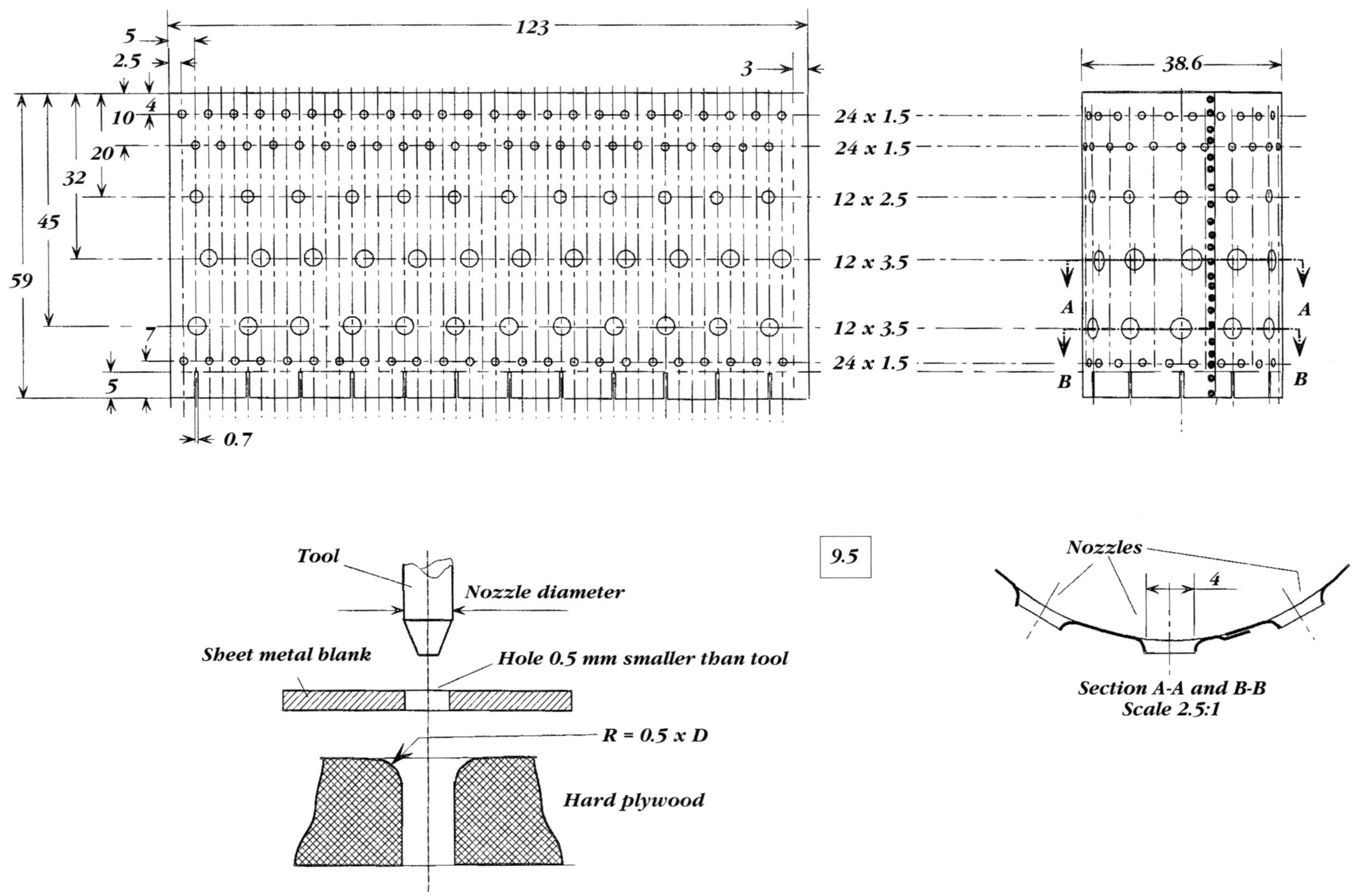

Sheet 10 of the drawings for the OHDIE 7 shaft power engine.

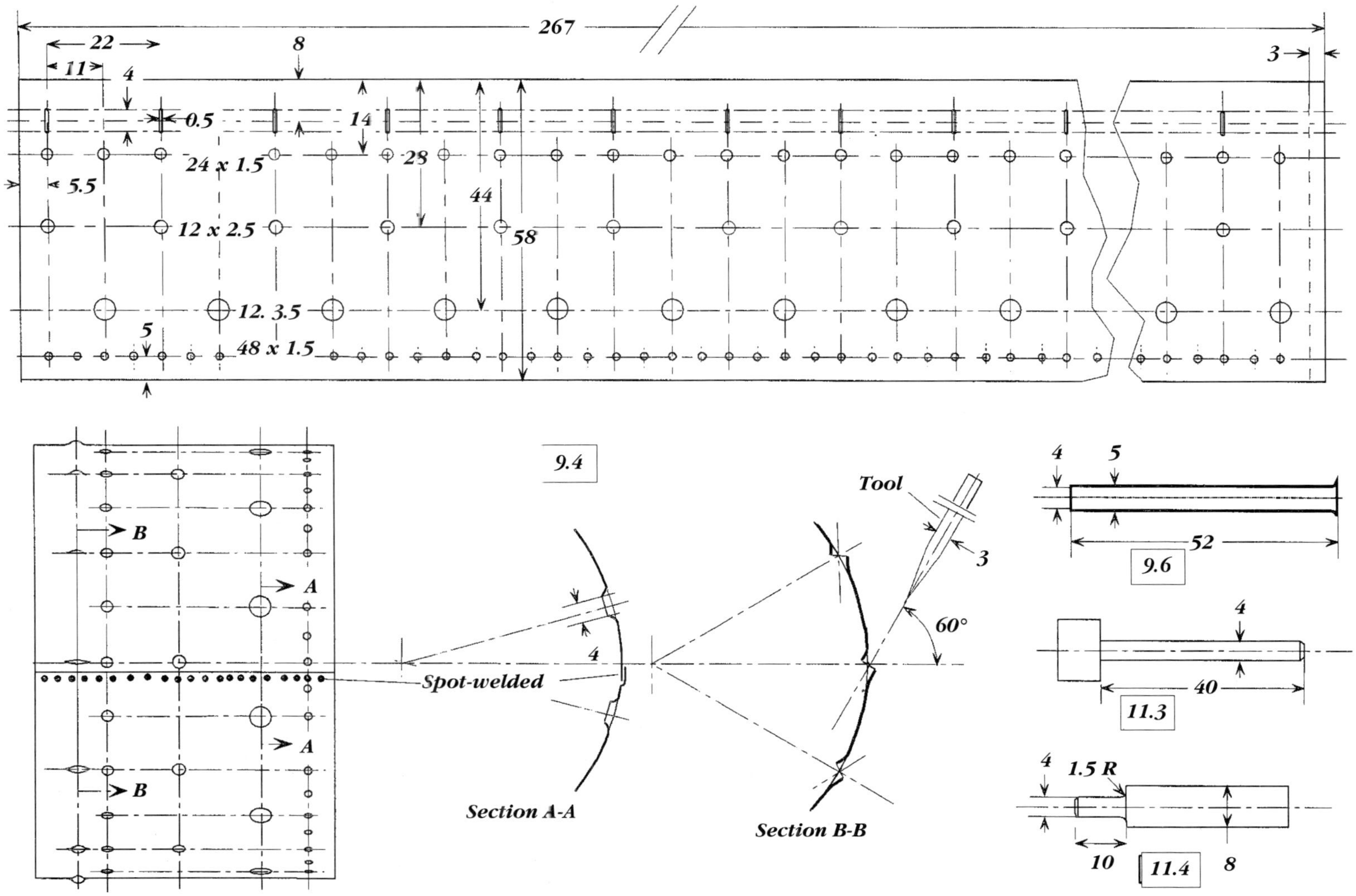

Sheet 11 of the drawings for the OHDIE 7 shaft power engine.

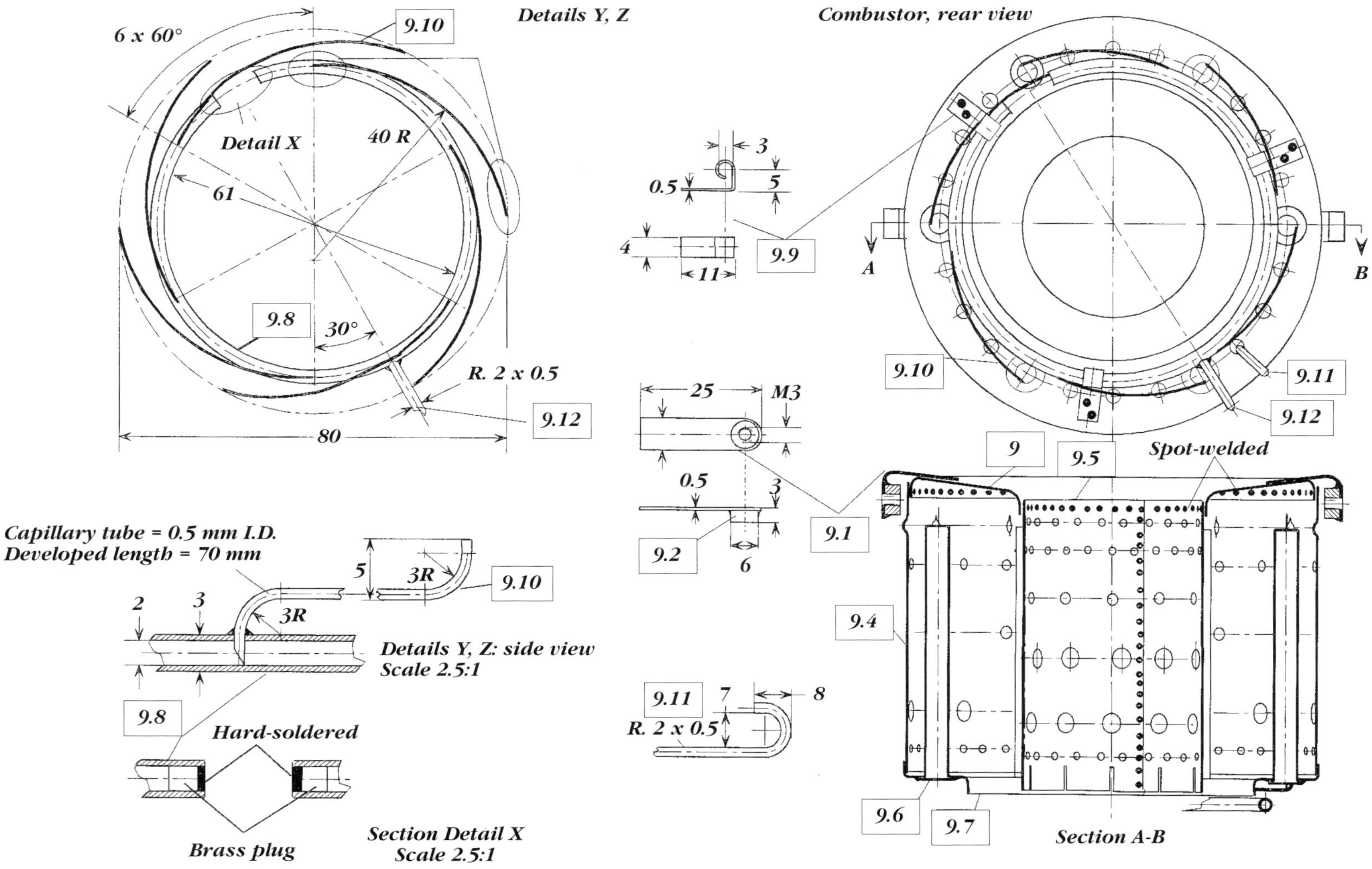

Sheet 12 of the drawings for the OHDIE 7 shaft power engine.

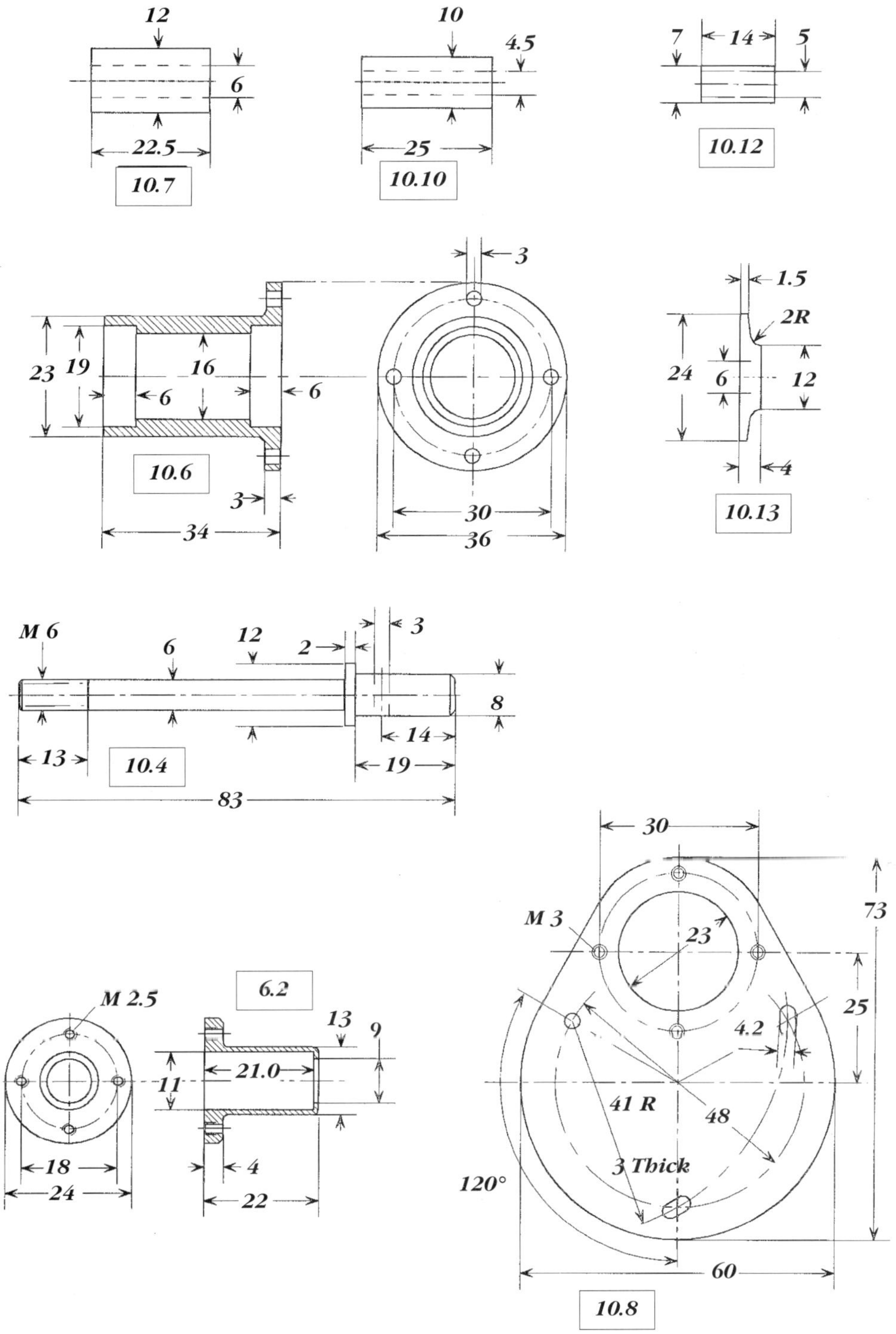

Sheet 13 of the drawings for the OHDIE 7 shaft power engine.

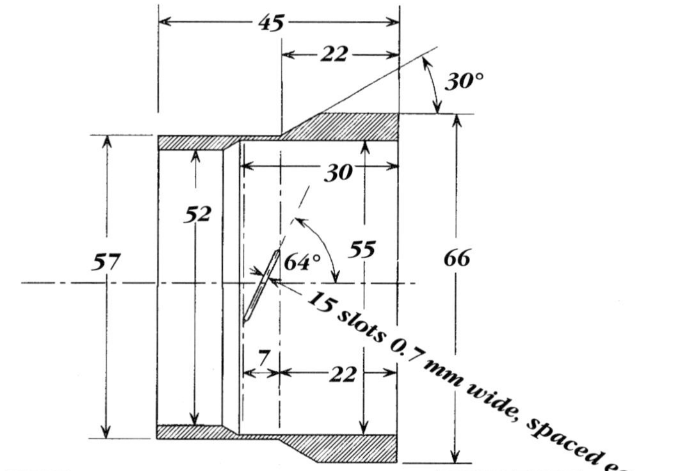

8 | ***Shape of part 8 before adding*** 8.1 | 8.2

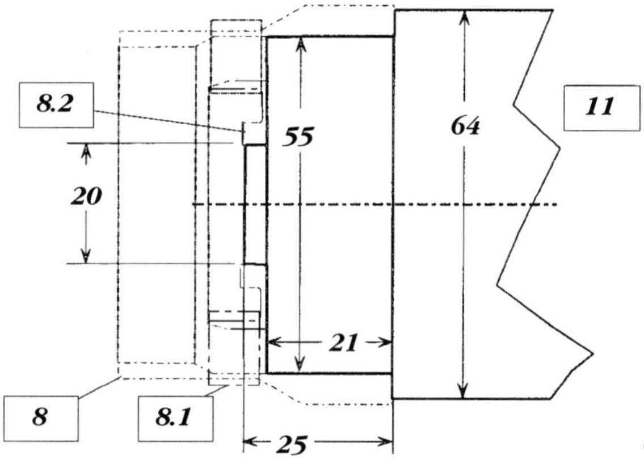

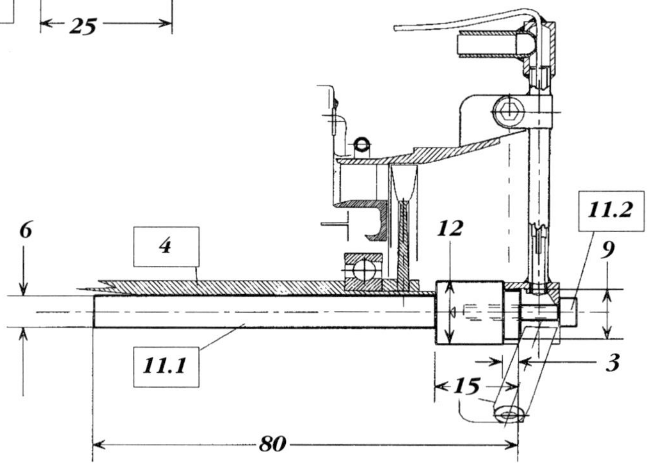

Sheet 14 of the drawings for the OHDIE 7 shaft power engine.

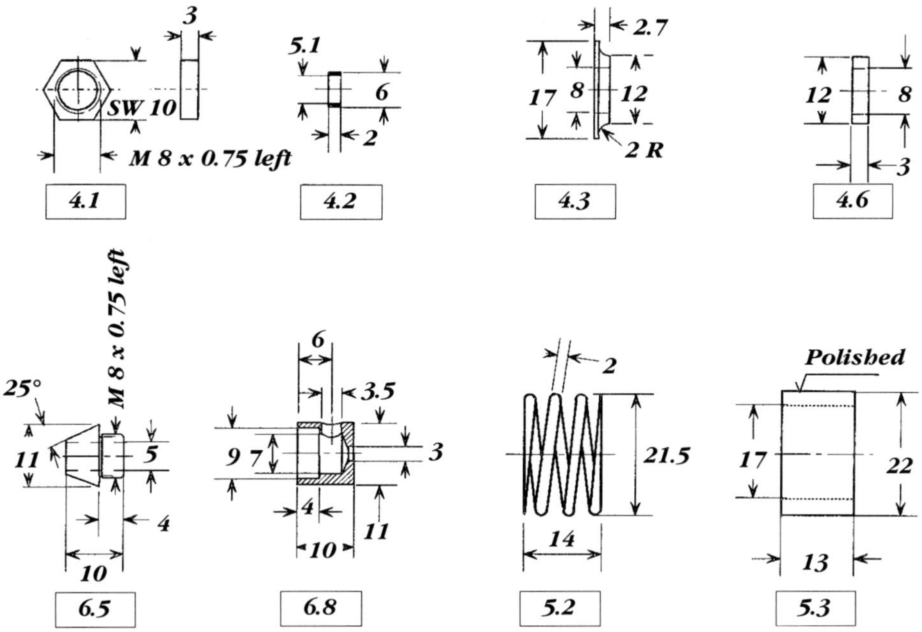

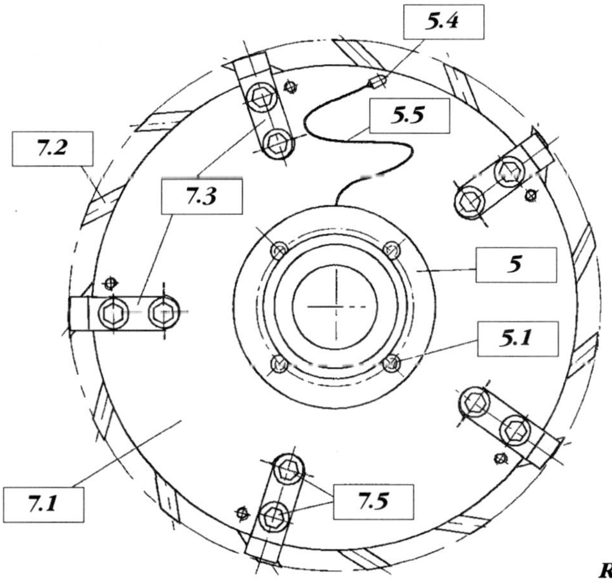

Rear view

Sheet 15 of the drawings for the OHDIE 7 shaft power engine.

Making the engine components

Engine housing, part 1

A wide range of manufacturers now produce seamless stainless steel containers for domestic use, and these form an excellent starting point for the engine housing. You will find a selection of them at reasonable prices in the supermarket or in household and hardware shops. The design of the engine requires that the housing should be at least 83 mm long, but this dimension is easily achieved by shortening a longer container. The housing shown in the drawing has an internal diameter of 94 mm, with a wall thickness of 0.4 mm.

As you would be extremely fortunate to obtain a container with exactly these dimensions, the design allows the use of tins with a diameter within the range 90 to 100 mm, with a wall thickness of 0.4 to 0.6 mm. Be sure to observe the following points if using a container of a non-standard size.

a) You will need to correct the dimensions of the compressor diffuser system components (parts 7 to 7.3) where they are attached to the housing. In all cases the external diameter of parts 7.1 and 7.2 should be 8 mm smaller than the internal diameter of the casing.

b) The internal diameter of the front cover must be adjusted to match the outside diameter of the housing.

c) The diameter of the outer combustor wall 9.4 should be at least 10 mm smaller than the outside diameter of the housing. If you have to adjust the size of this component, note that the hole spacing must also be corrected. If the internal diameter of the housing you intend to use is larger than 94 mm, you do not need to change the dimensions of the outer combustor wall.

Naturally, it is important to measure the diameter of the front part of the housing blank as accurately as possible, so that the mating sections of the components mentioned above can be made to a precision fit. First cut the housing blank to its proper length of 83 mm, then cut a perfectly circular disc of 10 mm thick plywood, with its edge tapered slightly. The disc should be sized so that its smallest diameter just fits inside the housing. Push the disc into the container, and it will be stiffened effectively and held absolutely circular.

Cut a 59 mm diameter opening in the bottom of the engine housing; this process is also best carried out on the lathe. The 3 mm Ø holes for the screws which connect the housing to the compressor diffuser system are made using the corresponding threaded holes in the connecting pieces 7.3 as a guide, i.e. they are not cut until the entire compressor diffuser system has been completed. The position of the elliptical 9 x 4 mm hole on the periphery cannot be established until the engine is finally assembled; the same applies to the holes for the pressure nipple 1.1, and for the starting air nozzle 8.3.

Round off the inside edge of the cut line at the front lip of the housing slightly.

Front cover, part 2

The ideal material for this component is a heavy-duty light alloy. Note that the inside contour at the front, leading to the diffuser vane intake, is not very critical, but in other respects the profile of the front cover should match the line of the outside edge of the compressor wheel vanes very precisely. When the engine is assembled, ready to run, the gap between the vanes and the front cover should be no wider than 0.2 mm, although 0.3 mm clearance is permissible at the front of the vanes.

The maximum internal diameter has to be selected to suit the outside diameter of the housing you are using; the permissible tolerance is +0.1 mm.

Don't cut the M3 threaded holes and the 2.6 mm Ø holes at this stage; they are made during the final assembly procedure, using the mating components as a guide.

Connecting piece, part 6.1

This part connects the front support for the power turbine shaft to the housing via the front cover.

This component must be made accurately, as it is crucial to the correct alignment of the power

Virtually ready-made turbine housings can be found in your local supermarket.

turbine shaft, part 6. It serves as mounting point for the gearbox, and also as attachment for a coupling to drive any other piece of ancillary equipment, e.g. a fan.

Initially the part should be machined on the lathe as shown in the drawing, after which the five openings in the periphery should be drilled out and filed to the shape shown in section A-B. Round off the struts and the front edge of the connecting piece using fine abrasive paper. Polishing these surfaces makes the finished engine look good, but does not affect the running qualities of the completed power plant. The 3 mm Ø holes are cut using the corresponding threaded holes in the front cover 2 as a template. Start by drilling through both parts using a 2.4 mm Ø bit, mark the relative position of the parts and dismantle them. The holes in the connecting piece can then be drilled out to 3 mm Ø. The holes which accept the gearbox must line up accurately with the gearbox itself.

Tubular shaft, part 4, and sealing ring, part 4.2

Special tools: long-shank 5.5 mm and 6 mm Ø drills, die for M8 x 0.75 left-hand thread.

The first step is to bore right through the blank, which should be around 15 mm in diameter; this is done on the lathe. The quickest method is to use the 5.5 mm and 6 mm long-shank drills alternately, in each case making about 20 mm of progress, starting with the 6 mm drill. Any attempt to drill from both ends using standard-length drills is guaranteed to go adrift, in the true sense of the expression. If your lathe does not include a cooling fluid feed system, turbine oil makes an excellent lubricant. Once you have drilled right through the blank, machine the part to the correct diameters and lengths, leaving them about + 0.2 mm oversize. The final work is then completed between centres.

The areas where the ballraces, compressor and turbine wheels fit should be turned down to +0.01 mm; the final fits are achieved by polishing the shaft at the appropriate locations. If you do not have gauges available, all fits involving the shaft should be a light press-fit. A loose fit renders the entire engine useless. A good substitute for the correct size of gauge is a precision ballrace, size 608. The flanged bearings which are used in the finished engine cannot be used as gauges, as they tend to fall apart quite easily if pushed in slightly off-centre axially, even when quite moderate force is used. Of course, the fine machining can also be completed with the help of a precision grinding machine if you have access to one.

The outside diameter and bore of the tubular shaft are not critical, and permissible tolerances are quite wide. However, it is very important that the central axes of bore and shaft are exactly concentric with the precision-fitted surfaces. An eccentricity of 0.01 mm is quite enough to make it impossible to balance the complete rotor adequately.

The M8 x 0.75 left-hand fine thread can be cut on the lathe if you have thread-cutting facilities.

The final stage on the shaft is to cut the 2 mm Ø vent holes which should run through the centre of the shaft; they should be as nearly symmetrical as possible.

The primary purpose of the sealing ring 4.2 is to seal the gap to the power turbine shaft 6. It should be machined on the lathe to form a press-fit in the tubular shaft. The part should not be fitted in the shaft until the final assembly stage.

Machining the compressor wheel, part 3

The recommended compressor wheel is a ready-made item, but it has to be modified for our purpose. Clamp it in a 50 mm collet, and reduce its overall length to 18 mm by machining metal away from the front. It also needs to be bored out to 7.8 mm Ø. This bore must be accurate, and we recommend that you make an internal gauge whose diameter is 0.01 mm less than the diameter of the tubular shaft 6 at the point where the compressor wheel fits. The bore can then be reamed out using an adjustable reamer until the internal gauge is an easy sliding fit through it. You should aim at obtaining a good interference fit in the rear third of the bore when the parts are assembled. At room temperature the wheel will then be a press-fit on the shaft. Fitting it on the shaft is very easy: just heat up the wheel in an oil bath to 120 to 150°C. If the wheel is heated evenly, the bore will enlarge by 0.018 mm if its temperature is increased by 100°C. Before you run the engine, the compressor wheel, shaft and turbine wheel must be dynamically balanced in the completely assembled state (see section entitled "Dynamic balancing").

Spacer disc, part 4.3, and spacer ring, part 4.6

The bore tolerance of these rings is relatively wide; 8H7 is accurate enough. The crucial point is that the front and rear faces should be exactly plano-parallel, otherwise the turbine and compressor wheels will not run true on the shaft, thereby causing dynamic imbalance. This is very difficult to correct by balancing.

Special nuts, parts 4.1 and 4.8

The easiest way of making these is to start with M6 machine nuts, which can then be bored out to 7.2 mm Ø prior to cutting the M8 x 0.75 left-hand thread. At the compressor end a heavy-duty light alloy could also be used, but for the turbine end nickel-chrome steel or better is required.

Shaft tunnel, part 5, with accessories, parts 5.2 to 5.5

Heavy-duty light alloy is suitable for these parts. The ballrace at the turbine end should be a light push fit in the shaft tunnel. When drilling the hole to take the oil feed tube remember to make it the correct diameter for the thickness of the tube you are using (0.8 to 1 mm Ø). The channel through which the oil passes can be cut with a mini-grinder and ball-nose cutter. It is important to ensure that oil can flow through the oil feed tube into the machined channel and then out of the front of the ballrace when the parts are assembled, complete with compressor diffuser system. The four M3 threaded holes in the flange should be drilled and tapped at the same time as the corresponding holes in the compressor diffuser system are drilled.

The thrust spring 5.2 is made from spring steel wire, and must be able to move freely inside the shaft tunnel. Making this type of spring is problematic even for the experienced model engineer, and the only solution seems to be to make repeated attempts, varying the diameter of the winding former.

Once you have a spring of the correct size, finish it in the usual way by grinding it on the flat face of a grinding stone, so that both ends of the spring form approximately flat surfaces.

The outside diameter of the sliding sleeve 5.3 should

slide easily, but if at all possible should not rattle. Its outside surface should be polished to ensure ease of movement. The rear bearing with sliding sleeve and spring is designed to provide an axial pre-load of about 40 N when the parts are assembled.

Silver-solder the lubricant feed tube 5.4 to the feed capillary 5.5 while the parts are still straight pieces of tube. They should be arranged as shown in the "Rear view" on sheet 15 during final assembly.

Power turbine shaft, part 6

If you use precision-ground round steel rod of 5 mm diameter for this part, there is almost no work to be done on it. Cut it to length, then machine the shoulder on the lathe to accept the ballrace. At the other end simply file a flat surface to engage the grubscrew 10.1 which secures the pinion 10.

Hub, part 6.5

The purpose of the hub is to connect the power turbine shaft to the power turbine wheel. The bore is of nominal 5 mm diameter, and must be accurate enough to be a press-fit on the shaft 6. The first step is to turn a cylinder 10 mm in length and around 12 mm in diameter. Bore it out to 4.9 mm diameter, and polish the bore surfaces. Polish the mating surface of the shaft 6 until it is just 0.01 mm larger than the bore of the hub. The hub blank can now be heated to about 300°C, and pushed onto the shaft in the correct position. Allow the parts to cool down, then continue the machining of the hub to the shape shown in the drawing. Cut the M8 x 0.5 left-hand thread as shown. It is important that the hub be made from non-alloyed or low-alloy tool steel if this shrink-fit is to be stable in the long-term.

Compressor diffuser system, parts 7, 7.1, 7.2 and 7.3

The compressor diffuser system is assembled from the diffuser vane holder 7, the base plate 7.1, fifteen diffuser vanes 7.2 and five right-angled connecting lugs 7.3.

The diffuser vane holder is prepared as shown in the dimensioned drawing on sheet 4. Cut the blank from 3 mm thick light alloy sheet, and drill a centre hole. Draw out a template for the diffuser vane slots, then glue it to

Compressor diffuser system before fitting the vanes.

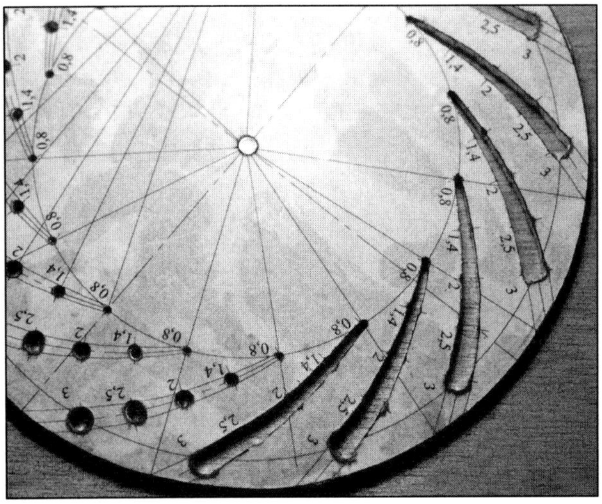

Preparation of the diffuser vane holder 7.1

A view of the completed compressor diffuser system.

the blank. The slots can now be sawn out using a piercing saw. Drill a centre hole and mark out the same diameter on the base plate. These parts can now be epoxied together, but first roughen the contact surfaces of the two parts using abrasive paper, remove all traces of grease, and finally clean them again using cellulose thinners or alcohol. Make sure that the prepared surfaces are actually the sides to be glued! On the prototype engines UHU Plus epoxy was used, cured in an oven at a temperature of 150°C as follows: pre-heat the oven, place the workpiece inside, then switch off the oven after ten minutes. When you have allowed the workpiece to cool down in the oven for 30 minutes, it is safe to remove it and continue working on it.

Centre the joined discs on the lathe with the help of the centring hole, then machine the front face of the diffuser vane holder flat, and turn down the outside diameter of both discs. The outside diameter should initially be left 0.2 mm oversize. The 22 mm diameter bore for the ballrace 4.4 can be cut by clamping the outside diameter of the disc, as shown in the dimensioned drawing on sheet 5. If the diameter of your engine housing 1 is not as stated, please note that the outside diameter of the finished parts 7 and 7.1 should be 8 mm smaller than the internal diameter of the housing.

The next step is to centre the workpiece on the shaft tunnel 5 using a standard 608-size ballrace (identical external dimensions to the ballraces 4.4 and 4.5), then drill the four holes for the M3 countersunk screws, and drill and tap the corresponding threaded holes in the flange of the shaft tunnel. The workpiece can then be screwed to the shaft tunnel, with the centring ballrace in place. For final machining of these parts on the lathe, clamp the shaft tunnel in the chuck using the ballrace for centring, as shown in the dimensioned drawing "Detail Z" on sheet 5.

Make the blanks for the five right-angle connecting lugs 7.3 as shown in the dimensioned drawing sheet 5 – leaving them oversize to accommodate the radiused area 47R.

The diffuser vanes can also be cut from 3 mm thick light alloy sheet; this is the procedure: start by curving the sheet material as shown in the dimensioned drawing, noting that the parts are not symmetrical. File the blanks to the wedge section shown in the drawing. Round off the front edge to a radius of 0.8 mm, and chamfer the rear edges.

The next step is to install the diffuser vanes and the right-angle connecting lugs, but first the excess epoxy must be cleared from the channels in the slotted disc. A good tool for this is a small hand-held grinder fitted with a miniature ball-end milling cutter. Any adhesive residues in the corners of the channels can be left there. Bore the ten through-holes and tap them M3. The diffuser vanes and right-angle connecting lugs can then be glued to parts 7 and 1 using the method described above, fitting the screws 7.5 at the same time.

Screw the diffuser vane holder to the shaft tunnel, with the ballrace holding alignment, prior to the final stage of machining on the lathe. The front contour and outside diameter of the diffuser vanes and the right-angle connecting lugs can now be machined to match the shape of the front cover 2 and the engine housing 1. The five M2.5 threaded holes are not cut until the final stage of assembling the engine.

Remove any excess epoxy in the spaces between the vanes using miniature grinding discs, and remove any projecting screw length in the same way. Polish the surfaces of the diffuser assembly. It is permissible to leave a fillet of epoxy in the corners with a radius of around 0.5 mm.

The size and position of the lubricant duct within the bore for the ballrace 4.4 are not critical. The only important point to note is that this duct must communicate with the lubricant feed tube 5.4 through the flange of the shaft tunnel.

Compressor turbine wheel, part 4.7

Unfortunately no ready-made turbine wheels of suitable size are available at present. This component is the part which is subjected to the most severe centrifugal forces. At the same time it has to withstand an operating temperature of 600 to 700°C at the blades, so there is no alternative to the use of a material which is extremely heat-resistant. The method of making this part is similar to that employed on the home-made FD 3-64 turbines, and which has also been used successfully by other designers, e.g. by Thomas Kamps (see bibliography in the appendix).

Extremely heat-resistant alloys are very difficult to machine. The most useful general-purpose tools are miniature abrasive discs based on silicon carbide and a high-speed mini-grinder. Hard metal milling cutters can be used with some success, but diamond-tipped tools are not a good choice. To bore the central hole cobalt-alloy drills of the HSSE type are required. HSS drills can usually only be used once, and even then they may spoil the workpiece.

The first step is to cut a disc of around 58 mm diameter from the sheet material, and then mark the position of the 17 blades on it. Next bore the centre hole; the disc should be a light interference fit on the shaft. Ideally you should use reamers designed for working extremely heat-resistant alloys, but if such tools are not available to you, cut a pilot hole using a 7.5 mm Ø HSSE drill, then machine out the bore using an HSSE cutter.

Shaping the blades starts by cutting the 17 radial slots, ideally using disc cutters 0.5 to 0.6 mm thick. The turbine disc is clamped securely between two 41 mm Ø steel discs. A steel claw tool can then be used to twist each blade through 20°, measured relative to the plane of rotation. Note the correct direction of rotation when twisting the blades, as shown in Section B-B. If the material you are using is thicker, you will not need to twist the blades through such a large angle.

The turbine blades now take the form of blocks, 2 x 9.8 mm in section at the periphery, 2 x 7 mm at the root. The blade profile can now be ground out as shown in the drawing sheet 8. Start this process using 1 mm thick fabric-reinforced mini disc cutters of 30 to 40 mm diameter. Smaller, thinner grinding discs are a better choice when you reach the fine shaping stage. The prescribed blade profile is not particularly critical, but it is important to reduce the trailing edge of the blades to as sharp a profile as possible. In order to be sure of adequate structural strength it is also important that the blade tip profile should be no thicker than the maximum of 0.5 mm, since lighter blades generate lower centrifugal forces when the engine is running. For the same reason (structural strength) the thickness of the turbine wheel disc should be tapered constantly, starting at 15 mm diameter and extending to 40 mm diameter, as shown in the dimensioned drawing. This work can also be carried out using the grinding tools previously mentioned. In fact, the turbine wheel can be used with this area left constant thickness, but the maximum permissible load is then significantly lower. I recommend that you start by making a test turbine wheel from 2 mm V2A sheet steel, as this can be used for gaining experience with the engine. Such a wheel can be used safely with compressor pressures of up to 0.4 bar.

The whole process of grinding produces a huge quantity of dust and grit, and therefore represents a health hazard, so a close-fitting dust mask with replaceable fine dust filters really must be used; cheap throwaway dust masks are just not good enough. Spectacle wearers are often tempted to eschew protective goggles, because they feel that one pair of goggles on their nose is already enough. However, the kinetic energy of the grinding particles which inevitably strike the spectacle lenses does a very effective job of etching the surfaces (I speak from experience)!

The outside diameter of the turbine wheel must be

finished to match the turbine housing 8, and to this end it makes sense temporarily to assemble the housing, the shaft tunnel and the shaft. The outside diameter of the turbine wheel should now be reduced until a gap 0.1 mm wide exists (use a feeler gauge to check this). Any final adjustment must be made during the test-running stage, once the parts have been dynamically balanced (see the appropriate section later in this chapter).

Power turbine wheel 6.6

Suitable material for this component is 3 mm thick Ni-Cr steel sheet (V2A-V4 or similar), as the maximum rotational speed of this wheel is only a fraction of that of the compressor turbine wheel, although heat-resistant steels can also be used. These materials are no stronger than V2A, but they are much more resistant to oxidation. If thicker sheet material is used, the turbine wheel ends up correspondingly heavier, and this reduces the upper rotational speed limit of the power turbine shaft due to resonance oscillation effects.

These materials can be worked straightforwardly using normal HSS cutting tools. The slots can even be cut using high-quality fine-tooth piercing saw blades instead of cutting discs.

The turbine wheel blades should be shaped as shown in the dimensioned drawing sheet 8, as described in the previous section. The wheel is screwed to the hub 6.5 by means of the M8 x 0.75 threaded hole (core hole diameter 7.2 mm), and this connects it securely to the power turbine shaft.

The final outside diameter of the turbine wheel can be machined on the lathe; it is permissible for the gap between the blade tips and the turbine housing 8 to be as wide as 0.3 mm. Naturally, this wheel must also be carefully dynamically balanced.

Power turbine shaft rear bearing

The rear ballrace 6.7 is mounted in the bearing sleeve 6.8, which is screwed to the bored lugs 6.18 by means of the two struts 6.9 and the combination strut 6.10. The combination strut 6.10 is attached to the corresponding bored lug using the clip 6.11. The combination strut 6.11 also carries the lubricant feed which consists of the capillary tube 6.16 and the connecting piece 6.13. The tube 6.14, which is installed laterally, feeds cooling air to the bearing via the air tube 6.15, and at the same time supplies lubricant via the capillary tube 6.16.

Heat-resistant material or Ni-Cr steel should be used for the struts 6.9 and 6.10.

The combination strut should be prepared as shown in the dimensioned drawing. As an alternative to the stepped bore it is also possible to press a sleeve of 2.5 mm internal diameter into a tube which you already have available. The important aspect of this component is that its cross-section tapers. Other sizes of tube can certainly be used; all you need to do is adjust the size of the clip 6.11 and/or the cross-hole in the bearing sleeve 6.8 to suit.

The bearing sleeve 6.8 is machined from a piece of 12 mm diameter steel rod, long enough to be held securely in the lathe chuck. The first step is to turn a cylinder of 11 mm diameter, then drill a 3.5 mm Ø hole about 3 mm deep, close to the front face and at right-angles to the centre axis. The combination strut 6.10 can now be hard-soldered in the hole, and the prepared struts 6.9 welded to it. The workpiece, with struts fitted, can now be clamped in the lathe chuck and the axial holes machined. The 9 mm Ø bore must accept the ballrace 6.7.

The dimensions of the capillary tube 6.16 and the lubricant tube 6.17 are not especially critical, since an additional method of lubricant metering is required in any case, which means that compensation can be made for variations in flow resistance.

The clip 6.11, the capillary tube/lubricant tube and the cooling air tube 6.15 are not installed on the engine until the final assembly stage. The same applies to installing the bearing with the help of the bored lugs 6.18.

Power turbine shaft front bearing

This consists of the ballrace 6.4, which is mounted in the bearing housing 6.2. The bearing housing is centred in the connecting piece 6.1 and screwed to it. The plain and threaded holes to accept the screws 6.3 are cut when these parts have been assembled, at which time their relative position can be marked.

Starting air nozzle, part 8.3

The starting air nozzle 8.3 is made from a length of 3 x 0.5 mm stainless steel tube. The actual nozzle is formed using a length of 1 mm Ø steel rod which is pushed into the tube. Crimp the end of the tube around one side of the rod using flat-nose pliers (see section E-F) sheet 7. With a little force the steel rod can then be withdrawn. Don't worry if you can see a slight gap where the tube has been crimped; that is not critical.

Turbine nozzle guide vanes system, parts 8 to 8.3

The turbine nozzle guide vane system consists of the turbine wheel housing 8, 15 nozzle guide vanes 8.1 and the inner ring 8.2. The wall of the turbine wheel housing is sufficiently thick to ensure that it acts as a burst-shield if a turbine wheel should suffer structural failure.

The housing is turned from the solid in two stages. Sheet 14 shows the dimensioned drawing for the first stage of machining on the lathe. With this procedure completed, the 15 nozzle guide vane slots can be cut. Note that the width of the cuts must be no more than 0.1 mm larger than the thickness of the vanes you intend to use. A spark erosion machine or similar specialist equipment is ideal for cutting the slots, but they can also be made using mini disc cutters and a small drill. Using the latter technique I recommend that you drill 0.7-0.8 mm Ø pilot-holes to mark the end-points of the slots before resorting to the grinder.

The inner ring 8.1 should not be cut to final shape until the final stage of machining, as shown in "Detail Z" on sheet 7. The first step is to machine the central 20 mm Ø bore. The slots are cut using the procedure described for part 8.

Make the 15 vanes as shown in the dimensioned drawing. If you are using extremely heat-resistant sheet material, mini cutting discs are again the best tools for cutting out and shaping these parts.

To assemble the vanes and the other two parts you will need the alignment jig A, part 11. The stated diameters ensure that the parts are a tight fit together. Now the vanes can be fed through the slots in part 8 and into the corresponding slots in part 8.2; note that the worked surface of the vanes should be visible from the rear. Rounding off the edges of the vanes makes this

The nozzle guide vane system before final machining.

stage easier. If the slots turn out oversize, and the vanes fall through, curve them slightly to produce a rear-facing camber in their worked surface. At this point you can adjust the position of the vanes until they project by roughly the same amount at both ends, and in this position weld them to the turbine wheel housing on the outside and to the inner ring using a TIG welder. MIG welding technology also works if that is all you have available; in this case you should use a spot-welding technique. It is not absolutely essential that the joint seams should be completely gas-tight. The only essential point is that the front of the joint lines at the periphery of the turbine wheel housing must be cleaned up in such a way that the combustor back panel 9.7 can be pushed on to a depth of about 3 mm without being obstructed.

The assembly is now ready for the second stage of machining on the lathe; clamp the whole component by means of the projecting 57 mm diameter section, and complete the shaping of the parts as shown in the dimensioned drawing. Drill the 26 mm bore in the inner ring.

Now all that remains is to cut the elliptical hole to accept the starting air nozzle: drill a 2.9 mm Ø hole through at right-angles, then open it up to the correct elliptical shape using a file. The starting air nozzle is installed during the final assembly process.

The final step is to open out the front edge of the nozzle guide vanes, using a pair of pliers with the edges of the jaws ground down to a radiused profile, with the purpose of enlarging the inlet opening between the vanes. Aim at widening the opening by 1.5 mm in the centre of the edges.

Combustor, parts 9 to 9.12

For the actual combustor, which consists of the front wall 9, the outer wall 9.4, the inner wall 9.5 and the rear wall 9.7, Ni-Cr steel sheet or heat-resistant steel containing 25% Cr, 20% Ni and 2% Si, is a good choice; the material thickness should be either 0.5 or 0.4 mm. The stated dimensions of the outer wall 9.4 are valid for an engine housing (part 1) whose internal diameter is at least 94 mm.

The first process is to spin the front and rear walls on the lathe to the shape shown in the dimensioned drawing sheet 9. You will need to make a spinning former, which can be machined from aluminium alloy or even hard plywood. The spinning tool can be a sealed ballrace with an outside diameter of around 30 mm. The ballrace should be mounted in a holder designed to be clamped in the lathe tool holder. Before using the ballrace, grind off the edges of the outer ring to a radius of about 2 mm. The acceptable tolerance for the diameter of the spun parts is +/–0.3 mm.

It is sensible to cut the holes in the outer wall and inner wall before rolling them to shape; the layout is shown in the dimensioned drawing sheet 10. You will encounter no problems in drilling the holes provided that you lay the sheets on a plywood plate into which the drill can continue. Carefully remove all rough edges from each of the drilled holes. You will also need to cut the twelve slots in the outer wall 9.4; the slots should be about 0.5 mm wide. A suitable tool is a piercing saw fitted with a metal-cutting blade. These slots are later re-shaped to form hooded openings as shown.

Some of the holes are re-formed to produce nozzles of 4 mm diameter; this is done using a piece of 4 mm Ø round steel rod, ground to a point at one end. To re-shape the holes the workpiece is laid on a sheet of hard plywood, prepared as shown in the sketch (sheet 10); drive the tool through the pilot-hole in the sheet material with a hammer. This process automatically achieves the correct nozzle radius and hole diameter.

With the preparation complete, the two workpieces can be rolled into cylinders, adjusting the inside and outside diameters to match the dimensions of the front wall exactly. Before you start rolling the panels, note that the nozzles in the inner wall must be arranged facing out, and those in the outer wall must face in. Spot weld the overlapped joints of the two cylinders. If you have access to a TIG welder, this makes a good alternative. The next step is to weld the inner wall to the front wall using the same technique. The twelve 0.7 mm wide slots on the rear edge of the inner wall should be cut using mini disc-cutters. The front wall can then be welded to the outer wall. Note that none of the welded seams needs to be completely gas-tight, as the completed combustor is an extensively perforated container in any case.

The combustor fuel feed system consists of the annular tube 9.8, the fuel tube 9.12 and the six capillaries 9.12, which are attached to the rear wall by means of the brackets 9.9 once the assembly has been completed. The first step is to bend the annular tube, which is made of 3 x 0.5 mm brass tubing, to form an open-ended ring with an inside diameter of 61 mm.

Next drill the six holes for the capillaries, plus the hole for the fuel feed tube. Blockages in the tube due to excess flux can be a problem, so take the trouble to cut the holes exactly the same size as the outside diameter of the capillaries and the fuel tube. The tubing to make the fuel feed tube should be around 120 mm long. Silver-solder the straight length of tube to the annular tube, then seal the open ends of the annular tube as shown in "Section detail X" on sheet 12, by silver-soldering brass plugs in place. A common mistake when hard-soldering Ni-Cr steels is to overheat the parts without feeding flux to the joint. In this situation the solder cannot flow, even though the working

This photo is worth a thousand words on the subject of spinning sheet metal parts. Here an aluminium cover for a model engine is being spun. The tool is a hardwood stick soaked in oil. The former is concealed by the cover itself.

temperature is correct. For this reason you should always heat the thicker brass tube first, then apply flux to the joint area, i.e. avoid subjecting the thin capillaries to the hot flame!

Grind the end of the capillaries at an angle as shown in the drawing sheet 12, remove rough edges, and solder them into the appropriate holes in the annular tube while they are still in their straight state. Silver-solder the joints. You can now clean up and de-burr the

The completed combustor in its finished form, before final assembly of the engine.

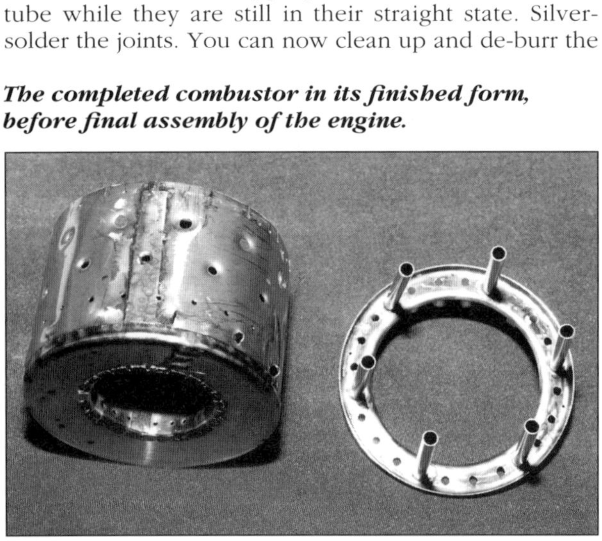

inside of the joints using a length of steel rod slightly thinner than the inside diameter of the capillaries. Miniature gas soldering torches are an excellent choice for these small joints. The best solder to use is a high silver content type with an external flux layer. Bend the capillaries to the shape shown in the dimensioned drawing before attaching the system to the rear wall of the combustor.

The sticks 9.6 are made from pieces of tube 53 mm long, and these should be belled out at one end using the tools 11.3 and 11.4 sheet 11 and light blows of a hammer. Cut the sticks to length as shown in the dimensioned drawing (also sheet 11), then insert them in the appropriate holes in the rear combustor wall 9.7 and hard-solder them in place. The sticks should be aligned with their centreline parallel to the axis of the combustor; and to this end you should temporarily attach the rear wall (complete with sticks) to the outer jacket. Fit a length of suitable steel rod into the sticks from the rear to help you align them accurately.

Bend the three brackets 9.9 just to the point where they can be fitted over the annular tube, and only then close them far enough to hold the tube firmly. Now position the annular tube relative to the rear wall in such a way that the ends of the capillaries project about 4 mm into the sticks, and rest against the inside surface. Hold the parts in this position temporarily by wrapping

Testing the fuel feed capillaries in their finished state with the help of butane gas. Equal flame length means equal flow resistance for the fuel.

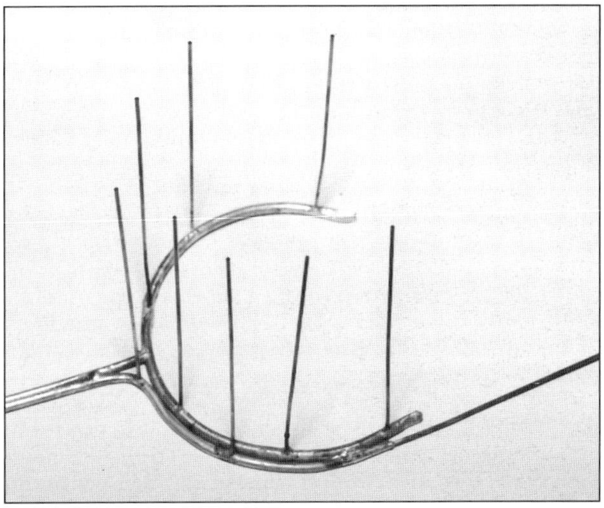

A different version of the annular fuel tube with feed capillaries. Here the auxiliary gas tube runs parallel to the fuel feed tube.

them with soft wire, then spot-weld the joints to attach the brackets to the rear wall. The rear wall can then be fixed to the outer wall by a few spot-welds, or with loops of stainless steel wire, for actually running the engine.

Bend the fuel feed tube 9.12 through 90° so that it faces forward, running parallel to the outer wall and about 1 to 2 mm away from it. Insert one end of the auxiliary gas tube through a hole in the rear wall, and fix it to the outer wall with a loop of wire. The brackets 9.1 and threaded bushes 9.2 can now be prepared; they are soldered to the front wall of the combustor during the final assembly process.

If you prefer to use a glowplug for igniting the engine, you can omit one of the brackets and use the threaded sleeve (¼") as the second fixing point for the combustor. In this case the threaded sleeve should be silver-soldered to the outer wall. The best location for the threaded sleeve is at the front, between two of the 1.5 mm Ø holes.

Gearbox, parts 10 to 13

The gearbox presented here is suitable for use with relatively small propellers. It was designed this way because of its intended location above the fuselage of the test model which was available. However, in general terms you can vary the reduction ratio to suit your preference. The gears used in this version are 35 teeth:15 teeth, modulus 1. Experience to date shows that a tooth width of 8 mm is adequate. The propeller shaft rotates anti-clockwise, as seen from the front.

The gearbox is supported on the connecting piece 6.1. The propeller shaft 10.4 runs in the ballraces 10.5, which are mounted in the bearing housing 10.6. The plastic gear 10.2 is connected securely to the shaft by means of the through-bolt 10.3. Axial clearance is provided by the spacer sleeve 10.7 which is longer than the distance between the ballraces in the bearing housing. The gear is connected positively to the propeller by the axial tension which is generated between the propeller driver 10.13 and the inner rings of the two ballraces when the propeller nut is tightened firmly.

The bearing assembly is screwed to the gearbox plate 10.8; radial adjustment is possible between the plate and the connecting piece 6.1. The two parts are joined by means of the three spacer sleeves 10.10 and the corresponding screws 10.11, and since two of the holes in the plate take the form of elongated slots, it can be swivelled around the axis of the third screw. This arrangement provides a means of fine-tuning the spacing between the pinion and main gear, which can be locked when the gears mesh correctly. The pinion is connected positively to the power turbine shaft during final assembly by means of the grubscrew 10.1.

Dynamic balancing of the wheels

Good dynamic balance of the wheels and their associated shafts is essential, but without specialised dynamic balancing equipment you need much patience, compressed air and a highly developed sensitivity in your fingertips. The fact that you have completed the construction process to this point proves that you have the latter facility. It is sensible to start by dynamically balancing all the parts separately after you have completed them, i.e. the turbine wheels should already be machined to their final outside diameter.

We will start with the dynamic balancing of the compressor wheel. The first stage is to determine whether there is any coarse imbalance in the component. Instead of the angular contact ballraces used in the completed engine, here we use standard ballraces of the same size, without seals and with any existing grease lubrication washed out using petrol. Use turbine oil or sewing machine oil as lubricant for the balancing procedure. Install the compressor wheel and tubular shaft in the shaft tunnel, complete with the bearings and spacer rings, but without the thrust spring and sliding sleeve. The whole assembly now has to be strapped down horizontally in some way. If you tap a metal rod on the shaft tunnel, the compressor wheel will rotate until its heavy side is at the bottom. Mark this point on the wheel, rotate it through about 90°, and repeat the procedure. If it again moves to the same position, you have certainly determined the heavy side. Cut a piece of fabric-based adhesive tape about 10 x 10 mm and apply it on the opposite side of the wheel. Turn the wheel through 90° again, and repeat the tapping procedure. In most cases this will produce a change in the position of the imbalance. Until this point the procedure has only enabled you to determine any coarse imbalance in the system. Fine correction using the fingertip method is the next essential step.

This is the procedure: remove the compressor wheel and shaft from the shaft tunnel, and fit one of the bearings used already on it, followed by a spacer disc. Now grasp the ballrace between the fingertips so that the shaft hangs down vertically. Direct compressed air tangentially onto the blades of the compressor wheel, initially from a fairly generous distance and at low air pressure.

Please note the following safety point: the blades of the wheels feature fairly sharp ends, and these can result in hand injuries when the rotational speed rises to more than 10,000 r.p.m., as is possible in the following test. Good protection is afforded by wearing leather protective gloves with two small holes cut where your sensitive fingertips hold the ballrace.

Once you have become familiar with the procedure, try applying the air at a higher rate and from closer range. If you are lucky, and the wheel is already perfectly balanced, you will feel no vibration through your fingers at all. If so, check that all is well by applying a small patch of fabric tape to any point on the wheel and repeat the experiment. You should now clearly feel the vibration; if you don't, then your fingertips are not suitable for this test. If all is well, you can move on to establishing the best possible balance, initially by mounting the wheel on the shaft in different positions, and then repeating the fingertip test. Be sure to mark the most favourable position of the wheel relative to the shaft, otherwise your good work will be lost.

Any residual imbalance can be detected by applying pieces of fabric tape of different sizes: repeat the compressed air test as previously described. Change the position of the balance mass, ideally applying it to the opposite point on the compressor wheel. If you can feel no difference, move the balance mass through about 90° and try again.

After you have found the point at which the balance mass shows the greatest corrective effect according to your fingertips, grind off a small sector on the flat face exactly opposite the balance mass, but only so far that the rear face is no thinner than 0.5 mm at the outside. Before applying the grinder be sure to wrap a piece of dense cloth round the ballraces to protect them. By changing the size and position of the balance mass, and grinding off material little by little, you will be able to achieve the best possible balance of the compressor wheel. Please don't be tempted to glue counterweights to the compressor wheel and leave them there while you run the engine. They are guaranteed to fly off, and the results may even completely wreck your engine!

You can consider the dynamic balancing procedure to be completed to a satisfactory level if a balance mass of around 5 x 5 mm of fabric tape produces a just detectable imbalance effect. If you don't have the patience to complete this procedure, I suggest you look for a different hobby.

The compressor turbine wheel can now be balanced to the same level of accuracy using the procedure outlined above. In this case any imbalance is corrected by grinding the blades on the heavy side to a thinner section. In most cases you will find that the vanes have turned out slightly thicker than those on the opposite side in any case.

The two wheels, complete with tubular shaft, spacer rings, thrust spring and sliding sleeves can now be installed in the shaft tunnel. For the next stage it is still permissible to use the standard ballraces which you have used so far for the balancing process. Use the fingertip method again to check the compressor end of the assembly, and then the turbine end. Mark on the wheels any fine corrections which need to be made. This calls for continued testing in the assembled state. From this point on the results depend very greatly on the precision of the ballraces you are using. To be entirely sure you should repeat the tests with the angular contact ballraces which will eventually be used in the engine. In order to test the power turbine wheel we need a temporary shaft tunnel into which the bearings will fit. The procedure described above is used to check its balance.

Final assembly

Adjusting the turbine nozzle guide vane system to fit the housing

The first step is to weld the turbine nozzle guide vane system to the engine housing. First press it into the housing from the rear as far as it will go. TIG welding technology is ideal for this, but MIG welding will also do the job. In this case you will need to spot-weld the parts together. To avoid burning through the material, I recommend that you machine a copper or aluminium ring at least 3 mm thick with an inside diameter of 61 mm, and press the ring against the weld point from the inside. This does not produce a particularly neat welded seam, but it fulfils its purpose.

Installing the starting air nozzle, part 8.3

Fit the starting air nozzle through the nozzle guide vane system from the rear, and solder it to the housing in such a way that the nozzle outlet is located approximately in line with the rear edge of the vanes. You will need to drill a 3.5 mm Ø hole at a suitable point in the housing to accept the tube. The free end of the nozzle tube can now be fitted with a suitable nipple.

Adjusting the compressor diffuser system to fit the housing

Push the compressor diffuser system into the housing as far as it will go, then drill the holes for the M3 screws through the housing and the connecting lugs, using a 2.5 mm Ø bit initially. For safeties sake mark the position of the compressor diffuser system relative to the housing; you can then remove the diffuser system, tap the M3 threads, and open out the holes in the housing to 3 mm diameter.

Installing the combustor

It is now possible to position the combustor accurately. This means that the gap in the annular tube must be located in the area of the starting air nozzle. The holes which accept the combustor lugs should be spaced 8 mm from the front edge of the housing, and can be cut at any point on the periphery. Remember also to cut the oval opening for the cooling air tube 6.15

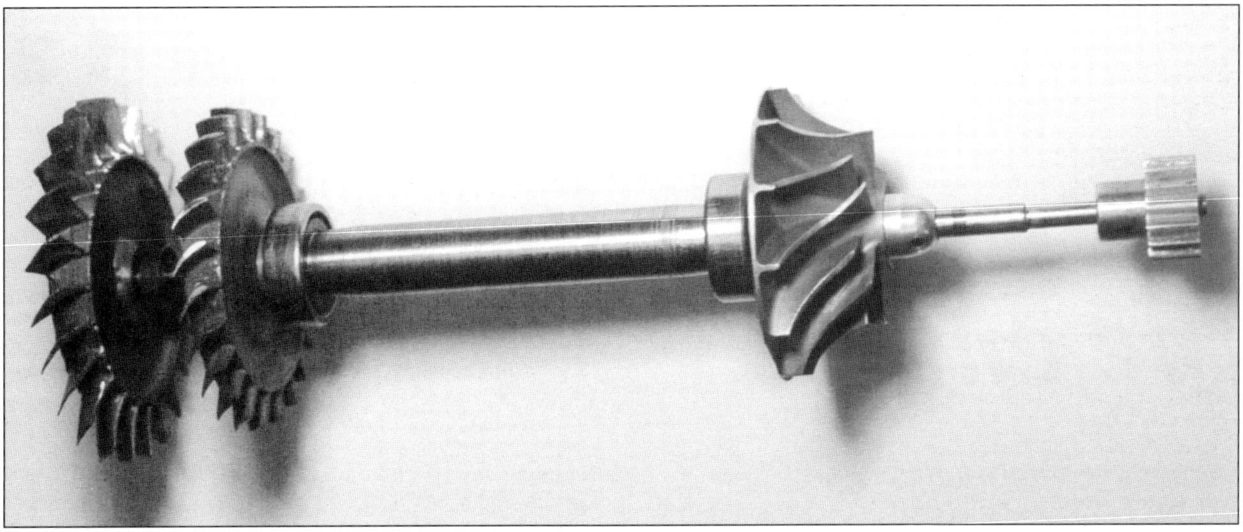

The two shafts of OHDIE 7, one running inside the other, showing the turbine wheels, ballraces and compressor wheel.

and for the pressure measurement nipple 1.1. The fuel feed tube and the auxiliary gas tube can be routed through holes in the compressor diffuser vanes, in the same manner as the front oil feed tube. Just determine the most favourable position for these tubes; it goes without saying that you should only choose those vanes which do not already feature threaded holes. These tubes can be bent to any shape within wide limits, so you can always find the most favourable exit position.

Once you have drilled the fixing holes for the combustor, use several wooden blocks to locate the component in the axial and radial position. The inside lugs can now be attached to the combustor, and the ends bent in such a way that they rest against the front wall. The lugs can then be hard-soldered to the front wall in this position.

Installing the compressor diffuser system

Fit the fuel feed and oil tubes through the appropriate holes in the diffuser system from the rear, then push the diffuser system into the housing and set it in the previously marked position. Fit the five fixing screws 7.4.

Installing the compressor rotor

Fix the tubular shaft in place together with the ballrace 4.5, the spacer ring 4.6 and the turbine wheel 4.7 by tightening the special nut 4.8; ensure that the parts are aligned in the position established during the balancing process. Fit the thrust spring 5.2 and the sliding sleeve 5.3 in the shaft tunnel, apply a few drops of oil to the contact surfaces, then slide the tubular shaft with the ancillary parts screwed to it through the shaft tunnel and the front bearing 4.4 from the rear. There is a danger that the inner ring of the front bearing will be pushed out when you do this, but you can avoid this by pushing against it with a length of tube with an inside diameter of 8 mm. Fit the ballrace 4.4 in the recesses between the base plate 7.2 and the shaft tunnel. Screw the shaft tunnel in place using the securing screws and thread-lock fluid. Push the tubular shaft through to the point where it rests against the inner ring of the ballrace 4.4. This action places the thrust spring under load. With the parts correctly located, position the spacer ring 4.3, heat up the compressor wheel to about 150°C and fit it on the shaft. The rotor can now be finally screwed to the shaft using the special nut 4.1. Press the sealing ring 4.2 into the tubular shaft from the front. Check that the rotor is free to rotate before completing the job by fitting the front cover.

The gap between the front cover and the housing can be sealed with silicone sealant or similar gasket material, unless the parts are already a tight fit. Allow the thread-lock fluid and sealant to cure, and the engine is then ready to be test-run on its own, i.e. without the gearbox and the power turbine shaft (see next chapter).

Installing the power turbine assembly

The first stage is to fix the connecting piece 6.1 to the bearing housing 6.2 and the ballrace, and to screw this assembly to the front cover 2. Instead of fitting the power turbine shaft, screw the bearing housing 7.5 and the screw 11.2 to the alignment jig 11.1 (see sketch on sheet 14), and slide this assembly into the tubular shaft from the rear. Fit the clip 6.11 on the combination strut, then silver-solder the distributor 6.13, the capillary 6.16 and the sleeve 6.14 in place. At this stage it is possible to check that the bored lugs 6.18 fit correctly, then weld them to the turbine wheel housing 8. Now undo the three screws 6.12 again, remove the alignment jig 11.1, and fit the power turbine shaft complete with power turbine wheel in its place. Check the gap between the blades of the power turbine and its housing, and if necessary correct the clearance; the permissible range is 0.2 to 0.3 mm. Locate the shaft axially by fitting the pinion 10 and tightening the grubscrew 10.1.

Installing the gearbox

The gearbox is fixed to the engine using the screws 11.1 and the spacer sleeves 11.10; set the correct meshing clearance between the pinion 10 and the main gear 10.2 as already described. Mount a suitable propeller on the shaft, and the engine is ready to be installed on the test-stand.

Chapter 13

Instructions for running the engine

Important safety notes

The following list of potential hazards which present themselves when handling model turbo-jet engines makes no claim to be complete. As we all know, human imagination is so wide-ranging that no single individual can ever cover all the possibilities, and this applies in particular to the unimaginable scope for making mistakes.

Here are one or two examples just to give you a taste: a modeller attempts to start a turbine by blasting pure oxygen into it instead of compressed air; another sees a drop of oil in the intake area and tries to wipe it away with a cloth; yet another offers his finger to the intake to see how powerful the suction of his engine is. All these basic errors have repercussions on the persons involved which they could hardly have imagined: turbines react very badly to a diet of concentrated oxygen, rags and fingers, and respond by destroying themselves – not to mention the finger concerned. I have not invented any of these crass errors! (Note: with a high concentration of oxygen the combustion temperature rises to around 3,000°C; hot aluminium or steel components go up in flames, producing a disastrously impressive fireworks display.)

Any turbine engine which is forcibly wrecked whilst running, regardless of the cause, is an object of extreme and incalculable danger. It is equally true that problems due to technical faults have results which are not 100% predictable. This means that, if you demand absolute safety, you must avoid all contact with such potentially hazardous technology.

If you have no practical experience in handling turbine engines, you should not consider test-running

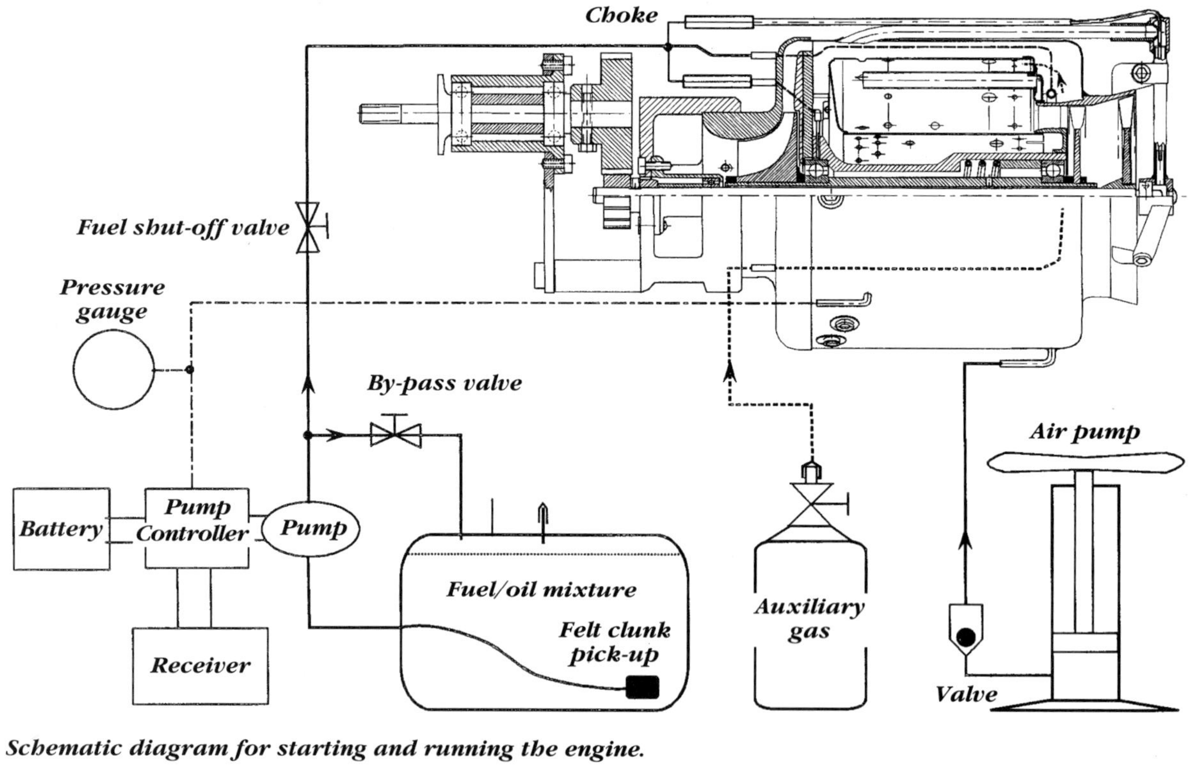

Schematic diagram for starting and running the engine.

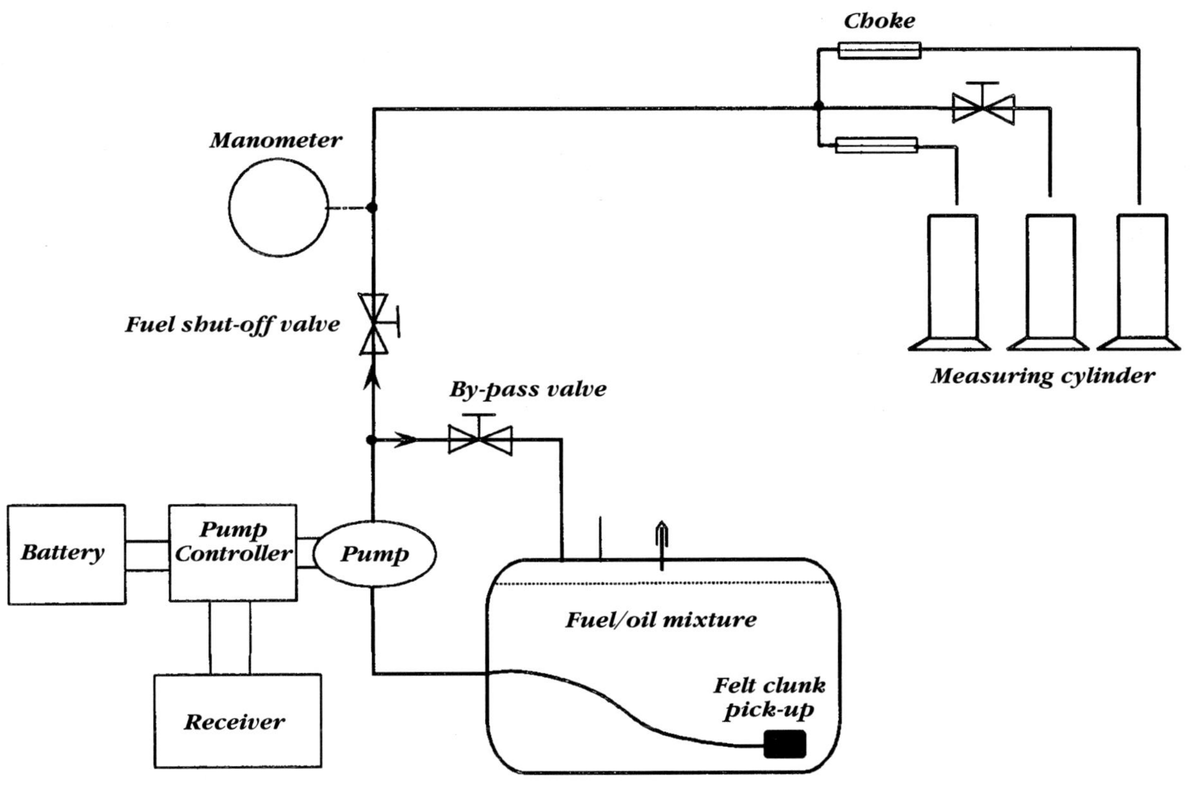

Schematic diagram for calibrating the chokes.

your new engine until you have obtained the assistance of an experienced colleague.

The following section explains the common dangers, which are by now more or less well acknowledged:

Fire hazard

As a basic rule, it is not possible to exclude the possibility of a fire outbreak on any model which carries a source of fire on board. Such potential fire hazards include: hot-running turbines, electric motors, piston engines and even short-circuited batteries. It is therefore advisable to abandon any idea of flying powered model aircraft if there is a risk of forest fire, or if there are fields of tinder-dry grass or stubble located close to the flying zone. However, the greatest risk of fire with turbine-powered models occurs during the process of starting the engine, and that eventuality can be covered reliably just by keeping a fire extinguisher close to hand at all times.

Ingested foreign body hazard

A particular risk to the engine is the ingestion of any foreign body; a situation familiar to full-size jet pilots as "FOD" (Foreign Object Damage). If the turbine engine is enclosed inside the model's fuselage, it is almost certain to attract any and all loose parts, and when it sucks them in the result will with equal certainty be FOD. It is also true that dirt and dust particles will be thrown up in the air by the turbulent airflow around the engine, which then sucks them in with gusto. This is a particular danger with tricycle undercarriage models whose nosewheel is located in front of the intake ducts, or with models whose undercarriage wells are not properly sealed from the internal fuselage cavity. Even puddles on the take-off strip may cause FOD, as water sprays up and into the engine.

Exhaust gas hazard

Up to a distance of about 1 m the exhaust gas is so hot that it will burn naked skin virtually instantaneously. The hot gas therefore works as a highly efficient igniter of such inflammable materials as dry grass, spilled fuel etc.

The volume of exhaust gas produced by a turbine is roughly the same as the exhaust from a medium-sized car at full-throttle. This means that it is not a particularly good idea to run a turbine in an enclosed space, or even in a poorly ventilated room; the oxygen you need to breathe (and stay alive) will be consumed in a surprisingly short time. Turbines must only be run in the open air!

The energy in the exhaust gas flow is sufficient to hurl small parts around at high speed, so never direct the exhaust jet towards spectators!

Rotating parts hazard

When running normally, a turbine engine's revolving parts are moving at very high peripheral speeds. If a wheel or propeller should suffer structural failure, the shrapnel will be hurled out in the plane of rotation, with impressive penetrative capability. To avoid personal injury please take the following measures to heart:

- Keep all spectators away from the rotational plane of the engine!

- If you wish to check the maximum power of a turbine engine, it should be done only on a test-stand, under radio-control, with no spectators!

- When you are using the turbine to power a model, never allow it develop the maximum power which you have established on the test-stand! The key to this crucially important safety measure is to limit the fuel supply to a safe maximum.

- Never exceed the maximum permissible rotational speed for the propeller, as stated by the manufacturer!

- Include a safety margin which allows for the rise in rotational speed in flight.

- If you are working with a turbo-fan engine, and if you are using a home-made fan, ensure that the fan housing is burst-proof.

- Don't make your own fan out of metal!

Incompetence/inexperience hazard

This is one area in which every modeller must make a responsible decision regarding his own competence. If you are the sort of modeller who enjoys carrying out maiden flights with any model aircraft before a large group of spectators, you are, in my opinion, grossly incompetent, not to say stupid.

Before test-running your engine for the first time

The diagram shows the basic set up for running the engine.

Adjusting the electronic control system to match the transmitter

The first step is to adjust the speed controller and the full-throttle setting on the transmitter in such a way that the controller is at "full throttle" just before the throttle stick reaches the corresponding end-stop. If the controller does not reach full-throttle when the transmitter stick is at its limit, it may be tempting to adjust the travel of that channel at the transmitter to correct the problem, but you must resist the temptation. If interference should occur, the controller may suddenly go to full power, in which case it will feed excessive fuel to the turbine.

The result may well be sudden and catastrophic overloading, with the destruction of the engine the most likely result, unless you have incorporated additional safety measures to limit the fuel flow.

The simplest method of avoiding this is to install a non-adjustable choke in the fuel feed line, designed to ensure that the load limit of the engine is never exceeded, even when full battery voltage is fed to the fuel pump.

It should be obvious that it is essential to set up the whole system on the test-stand, and to practise the starting procedure until you are confident.

Calibrating the lubricant metering chokes

Another drawing shows the basic arrangement for adjusting the chokes. I assume that your fuel includes 5% turbine oil. From this mixture 3 to 5% should be bled off to lubricate the engine, and it is the chokes which determine this proportion. The calibration process should be carried out at a pressure of about 1 bar, and this corresponds to a mid-range speed on the fuel pump, with the fuel shut-off valve part-open. If you do not have a suitable measuring cylinder to hand, you can use a capture vessel (not a yogurt pot!) and calibrate it by weight comparison. Run the pump for a about a minute, and you should find approximately 100 g of fuel in the central capture vessel; when the chokes are set correctly, you should find 3 to 5 g of fuel in the vessels under the chokes; if so, then the calibration is in order.

The starting procedure

As with any other combustion engine, supplementary energy is required initially to start the engine rotating, followed by some form of ignition to get the process under way in the combustor.

All model jet engines designed to run on liquid fuels, such as kerosene, diesel/petrol or similar, require the combustion zone of the combustor to be pre-heated in order to produce a mixture which can be ignited. Even if complex measures are taken to atomise the fuel finely and feed it into the combustor, ignition will not occur without pre-heating, even with the high temperatures encountered in an average Central European Summer; at least, not in my experience. The safest method of pre-heating the combustor is to start the engine running on propane/butane from a gas cartridge designed for soldering torches (known as the auxiliary gas method).

Immediately before you start the engine we recommend that you test the lubricant feed system. This is done by sealing off the fuel feed before it reaches the engine, disconnecting the chokes from the engine, and running the pump briefly at low power.

The starting procedure is a simple matter of routine; the following checklist and associated notes refer to the diagram and should make everything clear

1. Close the main shut-off valve.

2. Connect the compressed air supply or the air pump.

3. Apply compressed air, and check that the shafts rotate freely.

4. Switch on the receiver: the pump feeds fuel back to the fuel tank via the by-pass valve, and thereby purges the system.

5. Open the by-pass valve fully.

6. Set the transmitter throttle stick to idle.

7. Feed a gentle flow of compressed air to the engine, and at the same time open the shut-off valve on the auxiliary gas container, and apply the ignition source to the engine's outlet.

8. When ignition has taken place, switch the compressed air supply or air pump to full power.

9. Set the transmitter throttle stick to centre.

10. Carefully open the fuel shut-off valve, fuel flows into the sticks and into the combustor, the engine accelerates until it is running above the self-sustain speed.

11. Switch off the compressed air when the compressor pressure reaches 0.1 bar or higher. If pressure does not reach 0.1 bar, carefully move the throttle stick slightly in the direction of full-throttle.

12. Close the auxiliary gas valve, disconnect the auxiliary gas supply and seal the gas connection at the engine.

13. Move the throttle stick to the full-throttle position.

14. With the fuel shut-off valve now fully open, cautiously close the by-pass valve to the point where the engine is running at the desired maximum permissible compressor pressure.

15. Adjust the idle setting using the throttle trim lever to $\geq$ 0.1 bar.

An aircraft powered by four turbo-prop engines is a particularly impressive sight.

Appendix

Bibliography – recommended reading

Thomas Kamps: Model Jet Engines

This author has worked very intensively on the development of model jet engines, and his book contains all the information required to build a powerful jet engine based on a commercially produced compressor wheel designed for a turbo-charger. This design forms the basis for most of the jet engines produced to date by home-builders, together with many commercially produced jet turbines. Thomas Kamps is a practical modeller, very well versed in the theory of turbines, and presents the essential theoretical knowledge in an easily digestible form. The contents of the book are exactly as promised by the title.

Thomas Kamps: Radio Controlled Model Jet Guide

This book, richly illustrated with drawings and photographs, provides all the essential basic information required to produce your own RC model aircraft powered by a real turbo-jet engine. Primary subjects include model selection, from experimental to sophisticated scale types, engine installation, maintenance, starting and take-off procedures and flying characteristics.

Kurt Schreckling: Gas Turbine Engines for Model Aircraft

This book was a world's first in presenting all the information required to build a working model turbine engine with simple means. It includes detailed building instructions and full design drawings, and also addresses the technical and physical problems and solutions, together with methods for calculating the essential parameters for designing a model turbine engine which is a practical power plant for current model aircraft. Measuring techniques, analysis of the results, and extremely comprehensive practical information on flying models equipped with the FD3/64 jet turbine are all included, and these subjects are still highly relevant despite many advances in the area.

Apart from these books there is no specialist literature available on the subject of the model turbine engine. The books listed below represent just a small selection of the comprehensive specialist literature which has helped the authors Kamps and Schreckling to become experts in their field.

Willi Bohl: Ventilatoren. Vogel Buchverlag, Würzburg.

Fritz Dietzel: Gasturbinen kurz und bündig. Vogel Buchverlag, Würzburg.

Dubbel – Taschenbuch für den Maschinenbau. Springer Verlag, Berlin.
Der "Dubbel" gilt als Bibel für Maschinenbauingenieure

Wolfgang Kalide: Einführung in die technische Strömungslehre. Carl Hanser Verlag, München, Wien.

Sources of supply

Unfortunately there still exists no single specialist dealer who can supply all the parts, materials and accessories required for model turbines, so we must still cast around for certain specialised parts and materials from non-modelling sources. For example, domestic hardware shops can supply stainless steel blanks for the engine housing, and the local pharmacist can supply hypodermic needles which make good capillaries. A good source of suppliers and addresses are model flying events devoted to model jet aircraft, and that is also the best place to find other model turbine builders.

Standard ballraces, gears, light alloy sheet, brass and stainless steel tube are available from some larger specialist model shops and from electronic component suppliers. Special ballraces with ceramic balls are supplied by the firm of Gebrueder Reinfurt of Wuerzburg, Germany, (generally known as GRW) amongst others. Suitable compressor wheels are made by KKK, and these can be ordered from a number of contract engineering workshops which specialise in the repair of turbo-chargers. Their addresses can be found in the Yellow Pages.

Notes

Notes

Notes

Other Titles

RADIO CONTROLLED MODEL JET GUIDE BY THOMAS KAMPS
Model aircraft powered by real jet engines are fascinating machines, capable of climbing vertically, pulling loops of virtually any size and flying at breathtaking speeds. This book explains how to make a successful start in this demanding sport. It provides valuable help in selecting a suitable model and the best choice of engine, as well as how to install the turbine, auxiliary equipment required, fuel systems and everything you need to build and fly your own model jet aircraft. Well illustrated, this book contains a number of photos and drawings providing all the information you need to make your own radio controlled model jet aircraft and fly it successfully.

MODEL JET ENGINES BY THOMAS KAMPS
Full details and advice on the construction and running of gas turbines. It includes highly detailed and well illustrated building instructions which the advanced model builder can use to make and even design his own jet engine.

GAS TURBINE ENGINES FOR MODEL AIRCRAFT BY KURT SCHRECKLING
Kurt Schreckling's innovative model turbine designs have quickly become legendary. Any jet modeller's library is incomplete without this book. It explains how to build Kurt's turbojet motor, the FD3/64 and contains full construction photographs and working drawings. New chapters by Kurt on the FD3/67 LS 'production' motor, its operation, installation and maintenance are also included. At last, the exciting world of real miniature 'jet' powered aircraft becomes available for all.

RADIO CONTROLLED PROBLEMS SOLVED by Simon Delaney

SCALE CONSTRUCTION by Duncan Hutson.

BEGINNERS GUIDE TO MODEL HELICOPTERS by Peter Rieksts

SCALE MODEL HELICOPTERS by Sean Brown

SCALE ELECTRIC FLIGHT by Jonas Kessler

GEARBOXES FOR ELECTRIC POWERED MODEL AIRCRAFT by Dirk Juras

SCALE MODEL GLIDERS by Cliff Charlesworth

OTHER TRAPLET PRODUCTS
Traplet Publications Limited produce a wide range of specialist modelling magazines, books, videos and plans covering radio controlled aircraft, marine, military and car models. For information on the full range or to order a free catalogue contact:

UK OFFICE:
Traplet Publications Limited.
Traplet House, Severn Drive, Upton-upon-Severn,
Worcestershire. WR8 0JL. England.
Tel: +44 (0) 1684 595300 Fax: +44 (0) 1684 594586
Email: general@traplet.com
Website: www.traplet.com

USA OFFICE:
Traplet Distribution USA Limited.
3103 Tatman Court, Suite 105,
Urbana, IL 61802. USA.
Phone: (217) 328 4444 Fax: (217) 328 2450
Email: usa@traplet.com
Website: www.traplet.com

AUSTRALIAN OFFICE:
Traplet Publications Australia Limited.
Suite 11B, Southern Corporate Centre, 35-37 Railway Parade, Engadine, NSW 2233. Australia.
Tel: 0061 295200933 Fax: 0061 295200032
Email: aus@traplet.com
Website: www.traplet.com